IT PROJECT ESTIMATION

Software engineering is becoming more procedural and controlled, but the estimation of IT projects is still regarded as a "black art". *IT Project Estimation* shows why it doesn't have to be. In this concise, easy-to-read guide, author Paul Coombs provides practical, detailed advice on IT project estimation. He shows why accurate estimates are needed, the different estimating methods that can be used, and discusses how to analyse the risks in order to make appropriate contingency allowances. He also covers pricing and billing strategies, and how experience of previous projects can be leveraged. Central to the book is a template for a cost model that incorporates task estimates, schedules, staff roles and costs, risk analysis, fixed costs, billing, and cashflow. Template Excel spreadsheets are included on the accompanying CD-ROM and there is a supporting website at www.itprojectestimation.com.

Putting everything into practise, the end of the book presents a complete case study showing exactly how a simple example can be scaled up to a real-life problem.

If you are an IT manager, project manager, or consultant, this book is for you.

IT Project Estimation

A Practical Guide to the Costing of Software

Paul Coombs
London

CAMBRIDGE
UNIVERSITY PRESS

PUBLISHED BY THE PRESS SYNDICATE OF THE UNIVERSITY OF CAMBRIDGE
The Pitt Building, Trumpington Street, Cambridge, United Kingdom

CAMBRIDGE UNIVERSITY PRESS
The Edinburgh Building, Cambridge CB2 2RU, UK
40 West 20th Street, New York, NY 10011-4211, USA
477 Williamstown Road, Port Melbourne, VIC 3207, Australia
Ruiz de Alarcón 13, 28014 Madrid, Spain
Dock House, The Waterfront, Cape Town 8001, South Africa

http://www.cambridge.org

First published 2003

Printed in the United States of America

Typefaces 10.75/13.5 pt. Berkeley Oldstyle and Franklin Gothic   *System* LaTeX 2_ε [TB]

A catalog record for this book is available from the British Library.

Library of Congress Cataloging in Publication Data
Coombs, Paul.
  IT project estimation : a practical guide to the costing of software / Paul Coombs.
    p.   cm.
  Includes bibliographical references and index.
  ISBN 0-521-53285-X (pbk.)
  1. Computer software – Costs.   I. Title.
 QA.76.76.C73 C66   2003
 005.3 – dc21   2002191142

ISBN 0 521 53285 x paperback

*T*o Logibods everywhere.

About the Author

Paul Coombs has been involved in numerous software design and implementation programs during his twenty-five professional years at the London-based systems house, Logica, and at the media organization, Reuters. He has worked on mission-critical developments for EMI, London Underground, IBM, the BBC, British Airways, and a large number of financial institutions. He has more than fifteen years of experience in the estimation and costing of large fixed-price projects in industry sectors as diverse as finance, defence, government, media, and communications. He is currently an independent consultant, providing educational services in estimation, proposal-writing, and bidding techniques, as well as cost/benefit analyses and proposals for specific projects.

Contents

Chapter 3
Estimating Each Task   **29**

Chapter 4
Planning the Project   **56**

Chapter 5
Analysing the Risks   **72**

Chapter 10
Case Study 128

Chapter 11
The Cost Model Template 147

Chapter 12
References and Resources 158

Index 165

CHAPTER 1

Introduction

For which of you, intending to build a tower, sitteth not down first, and counteth the cost, whether he have sufficient to finish it? Lest haply, after he hath laid the foundation, and is not able to finish it, all that behold it begin to mock him, saying, This man began to build, and was not able to finish.

—*Luke 14:28–30*

ARE YOU ESTIMID?

No one wants to do the estimates. It is the most thankless task our industry can impose—an enormous responsibility for a difficult and highly speculative job. An unsuccessful estimate can result in long hours for the project team; sticky explanations to managers and customers; and, above all, enormous financial loss. If a project loses a million dollars, it might take ten million dollars worth of successful work to regain the break-even point. Everybody remembers the name of the person who costed a disaster, but no one ever recalls the genius whose prediction was correct to the day, for success will be attributed to the abilities and dedication of the development team. If you want glory: don't do the estimates.

So there is an understandable reluctance for anybody ever to provide any estimates. Most people will vacillate; delegate; or even, as a last resort, flatly refuse to provide a credible set of figures with their name appended. I call this attitude **estimidity**. In this book, I discuss how estimidity is revealed and how it can be overcome. My aim is not to define some algorithmic method to obtain reliable estimates—indeed, it is my belief that no such method exists or will ever exist. Instead, my goal is to make you feel good about your own estimates by ensuring that they are the best that could be done at the time.

Bad estimates mean that good projects don't start, but land us with the impossible ones. So banish estimidity and tackle the task with thought and method to the best of your ability. No one can ask for more than that.

WHY ARE ESTIMATES SO BAD?

When I told some friends—all well-seasoned project managers—that I was writing this book, I was treated with some scepticism. "Things take as long as they take" was the general view. "All IT projects go over budget—it's just their nature." My friends all have plans, timetables, risk analyses, change control procedures, and the other manifestations of a well-managed project in place, but are cheerfully resigned to exceeding its estimated time and budget and to limiting the amount of the proposed functionality to be implemented.

They are not alone. The 2001 British Computer Society (BCS) Review revealed that of 1,027 projects surveyed, only 130 were successful—success being defined as delivering everything specified, to the quality agreed on, and within the time and costs laid out at the start. Of 500 development projects (rather than maintenance or data conversion), only 3 succeeded. In the United Kingdom, many recent public-sector IT ventures have ended as high-profile fiascos, but the story is similar in the private sector, in the United States, and in the rest of the world (see Chapter 12, "References and Resources", for more surveys).

Is all this down to poor estimation? We can divide the failures into two classes. Firstly, there are those where the rot had set in before the project even began—usually because it never was the right thing to do in the first place. Although this sad truth may emerge only midway through the development, we can't pin the failure onto bad estimation. But the second group are those projects which *could* have succeeded, but where the initial estimates disregarded the foreseeable risks. Most of the failure factors cited by project managers in the BCS survey are risks that they neglected to budget for—uncontrolled changes, unrealistic client expectations, open-ended third-party contracts, unexpected data conversions, complex interfaces, and so on. If risk is not eliminated in advance, it must be included in the budget. Instead, every time, the failure factors were encountered as a total surprise, and the project was derailed.

Why do we keep on making the same mistakes? I believe it is because underestimation is now expected and acceptable. If we costed projects properly,
for example by adding sufficient contingency to cover all the risks, pricing staff
at their real cost to the organisation, and including the running costs of the
completed system, then most would never start; they could not be justified. But
everyone *wants* new projects to start. Managers have revolutionary ideas; there
are business opportunities that can't be missed; and, let's face it, designing new
systems is far more interesting than maintaining the old. And as for asking some
consultants, well, of course they think you should proceed—indeed, they will
often quote you a price below their cost, secure in the knowledge that there will
be sufficient changes to recoup the initial loss. The friends I mentioned earlier
started their projects *knowing* that success was unlikely, and possibly not even
expected, so they are not striving overmuch to achieve it. They see their job as
one of damage limitation.

Here's some proof. Several years ago, I undertook an analysis of the fixed-
price projects undertaken by a large software house. The results are summarised
in Figure 1.1. Some of the projects made large profits, and some made large
losses, but most clustered around the break-even point. At first sight, this may
seem fine—the majority of projects completed for somewhere near the cost
estimated. But the Y scale is the profit, not the cost. The software house added a

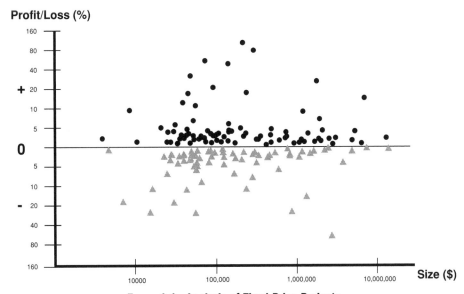

FIGURE 1.1. Analysis of Fixed-Price Projects

mark-up and a contingency allowance in order to derive the fixed price quoted to the customer. So the chart shows that most of these projects ate all the time estimated, ate all their contingency allowance, and finally ate all the potential profit before stopping. What has applied is a corollary to Parkinson's Law: The work has contracted to fit the budget available. How? By reducing the functionality, the quality, or both. As the bottom of the pot was reached, the more accurate the cuts became, so each project eventually delivered something just about acceptable for the price.

There are many conclusions we can draw from this chart. "Stop doing fixed-price projects" is one, for there seems to be no profit in them. And "don't bother with estimates" is another, for it appears that most projects will deliver *something*, regardless of the allocated budget. But what the chart really demonstrates are the points I have already made—most projects are underestimated to start with, insufficient allowance is made for predicable risks, and the only option left to project managers is to take an axe to the requirements. Underestimation may not explain every outcome, but if all the dots on the chart were raised upwards by a few notches, the software house would be undertaking work that yielded a consistent and predictable profit, and their customers would receive the functionality and quality they specified. Accurate estimates get us what we all want, but over-optimistic figures dreamed up to make a sale, to force through a pet idea, or to meet artificial delivery targets eventually lead to compromise.

Many years ago, I watched as a nuclear power station was constructed in one of my favourite parts of the countryside. The project was meticulously planned. The team did not dig a huge hole in the ground and then say, "Hmm, what shall we do now? Nuclear, gas, or coal-fired? Pressurised water or gas-cooled?" No— only *software* engineers work like that. "Let's build the easiest, cheapest, flashy, interesting, beneficial, cost-effective, or quickest bit first" has come the cry from a thousand different projects, "and we'll worry about the rest later." I have lost count of the times I have costed a system "properly" only to have that figure butchered in order to justify commencement. How often have we started on "phase one of phase one"—a project yielding no business benefit in itself, but one that allows us to make a start on a larger initiative for a low cost? And how many times have we then found that because that project yielded no benefit, obtaining the funding for the next phase became impossible, and the initiative flopped?

We need to get real. The purpose of an estimate is not to come up with a price that will get the project off the ground. So let's examine why we really need to undertake this thankless task.

WHY ESTIMATE?

Estimates are needed for three principal reasons:

1. To justify a project—enabling the cost to be compared with the anticipated benefits, and "what if" assessments to be undertaken in order to choose between different technical, environmental, or functional options.
2. To act as the central element of software engineering practice—enforcing the discipline to make the project succeed.
3. To improve the software production procedures—evaluating the effects of process improvements.

I expand on each of these in turn.

Justifying the Project

I once undertook some work for a large organisation that initiated new business process reengineering programmes after each management shake-up. No justification was attempted—the organisation did not maintain the underlying figures to allow costs or benefits to be assessed. Instead, the gut feel of the new architect of change was sufficient. The initiative would potter along for a year or two, and then the sheer volume of work, and the associated costs, would suddenly become apparent. The programme would be halted and then renamed, and soon there would be another management shake-up, allowing the cycle to begin again. That organisation is now in crisis because it has not modernised its business model, despite the expenditure of countless millions on projects intended to do so. A familiar story, with a simple moral—*estimation saves money*. In this case, it would have been difficult and expensive (the first time) to analyse the costs and benefits of any proposed initiative, but well worthwhile in order to save the money wasted on work that could not be justified.

For projects can only be justified if they are cost-effective and timely. If a new system saves one million dollars a year but costs forty million dollars to develop, it's probably not going to be approved. If the software has to display the election results or control a satellite, it better be finished on time or the entire effort will be wasted. I can think of very few cases in history where a major engineering development took place with no regard to cost or time. Even while the Great Pyramid was being planned I'm sure that someone wanted to know if the expense was justified and that they continued to question this while the effort mounted and the timescales lengthened. The business, organisational, and technical environment will inevitably change as the project proceeds, so there may be a point at which continuation is no longer worthwhile. By undertaking an honest, unbiased estimate we can see if it is sensible even to begin, and if we keep this view of the costs and benefits up to date, we can see if it is worthwhile to carry on.

This book concentrates on costing. If you want to decide if your project should or should not go ahead, or whether a change is justified, you also need to evaluate the benefits. And you must be able to do that using a measurement that is directly comparable with the cost: money. It may seem difficult to estimate the cost of a software application, but estimating the benefits it brings in cash terms is often even harder. How many more people will buy our product if it has this extra feature? How many will stop using it if the feature is not implemented? But there is no point in estimating the project cost to the nearest cent if this is going to be compared with someone's gut feel of the benefits. Improvements to the costing of proposed projects must go hand-in-hand with improvements in determining their benefits.

Engineering the Development

At the nuclear power station, the engineers did not complete the reactor and then decide to order some fuel rods, which take three years to make. They didn't complete the roof first and then start on the walls. The work of the different teams had to be synchronised, equipment and components had to arrive at the anticipated time, and operational staff had to be trained and ready—just as for most IT projects. If each of these parallel strands is not predicted and controlled, the timescale will start to stretch, and the costs to rise.

Software development is an engineering task. Sometimes highly skilled and motivated technical teams do manage to craft innovative systems with the minimum of process and planning, but the rest of us need a disciplined framework within which we can make progress. This means establishing processes for requirements management, change control, progress assessment, testing methodology, and all the other elements of the development life cycle. Even if incremental techniques are being used, there must be an engineering approach within each cycle, or we end up with technical anarchy.

So where do estimates fit into the engineering paradigm? Everywhere. You can't manage what you don't measure, and to measure something you must have a standard to measure against. So at every stage of the project engineering life cycle, from the vague concept to the post-mortem, an up-to-date model of the anticipated time and cost is needed in order to direct the team and to inform the customers. Without estimates, you do not have such a model. Its purpose is not make the project finish any earlier but to allow everyone to see what has happened, what is happening, and—most importantly—what is yet to happen. We must start with an initial estimate—our model of the cost and timescale of the project—calibrating and maintaining this as development proceeds and the inevitable problems and changes are encountered.

For during software engineering projects, it is taken for granted that serious changes to the functionality can be introduced at any stage, while still maintaining the same timescale. Civil engineers would not alter a bridge design from suspension to cantilever while halfway across, but IT project managers are well used to changes just as fundamental. The British Computer Society review found that 76.3 percent of project managers reported that they had *never seen* an IT project delivered in accordance with its initial specifications. How do our designs get so out of control? Obviously, one reason is simply that you *can* alter software specifications more readily than bridge blueprints. And the environment into which IT systems are delivered changes more quickly than the equivalent for bridges. But the most significant reason is that we so rarely evaluate the cost of a proposed change or how much benefit it will bring. Instead, we depend on someone's gut feel that it is the right thing to do. It is *because* it is possible to change IT projects so easily that we need estimates. They give us some ammunition—some real facts—with which we can evaluate whether a particular development, or a proposed modification, is justified.

Improving the Process

Other engineering disciplines have managed to introduce predictability through the sharing of experience, standardisation, and modelling. For example, although some civil engineering projects (such as the Channel Tunnel) are unique, high risk, and prone to overruns, most (such as apartment blocks and bridges) are completed on time, within budget, and don't keep falling down once delivered. But software engineering projects all seem to be of the overrunning, falling-down-afterwards type. We should be getting better, utilising component-based and off-the-shelf solutions, but we still seem to come up against the same old difficulties, both technical (e.g., communications, integration, and testing) and organisational (e.g., customer expectations, change management, and third parties). And we never learn. If an aircraft crashes or a bridge collapses, there is an investigation, a report, and the whole industry learns a lesson. Software engineering disasters are just written off, explained away, and then ignored.

We need to come out of denial. By measuring how long a project takes, comparing this against the original estimates, and analysing the differences, we will improve our techniques for estimation. And we can then see, in a tangible form, the results of using new tools and methods. Every organisation needs metrics in order to assess how well they are doing against expectations. In an organisation where IT projects play an important role, the metrics associated with those projects are particularly essential. So collect them. You will then have the tools to improve the predictability of IT initiatives, while your competitors will continue to cover up the disasters, ignore the lessons, and repeat the same mistakes.

Is Estimation Possible?

There are twelve **Blindingly Obvious Rules of Estimation** defined in this book. I have called them that because they are not rocket science, not precise results from years of academic research, and not even truths only someone as experienced as myself could have realised. They are rules we all know. Of the twelve, Rule 1 is not only the first but also the most fundamental.

Blindingly Obvious Rule of Estimation Number 1
Your estimate will be wrong.

How can it be otherwise? You are being asked to predict the future. And it is not the future of something with so limited a count of contributory factors and end results as a horse race. It is an IT project—an undertaking that may encounter any number of events that will affect its progress, change its scope, and challenge its entire reason for being. No one can foresee what will happen to such a beast.

Even if you implemented the same project several times over, it would take a different course each time. So, when you think about it, the project duration is not a fixed number but a statistical entity, as shown in Figure 1.2. There is a minimum time the project could possibly take, which is why the standard bell curve is skewed. But there are so many events that may happen along the way that we could never predict the maximum duration. So estimation—or at least

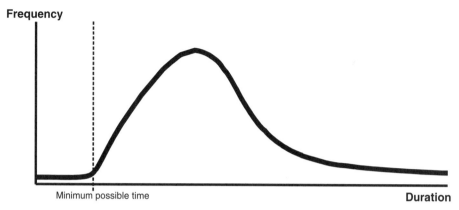

FIGURE **1.2. Frequency of Possible Project Durations**

100 percent accurate estimation—is not possible. You could pick a number and be lucky, but in a parallel universe, fate would take a different course and that number would be wrong.

Despite this, we can use our best judgment, taking into account every fact and every doubt we have, to produce the most likely figure that can be predicted at the time. But don't ever convince your management, your customers, or yourself that this number is going to be precise to the day or to the dollar.

WHAT'S WRONG WITH OVERESTIMATION?

Estimidity encourages the belief that it is never wrong to overestimate. But this pretty much guarantees that new projects will never start or, in a commercial environment, that you will never win any new work. It may not be your decision to withhold the go-ahead, but if you have padded the estimates just to protect your back then you will bear responsibility for the failure to achieve the benefits that the project could have delivered.

In IT's early days, the management of large software projects was somewhat hit-and-miss because the drivers behind success or failure were unknown and unpredictable. Overestimation was common, because profitability could still be achieved even if there was time to draw a few "Snoopy" calendars along the way. Today's world is more competitive, and organisations can no longer afford to finance projects that will *easily* run to time and budget. So we need precision in our estimates, not just the figure for which we can say, "it can't possibly take longer than that."

WHO SHOULD DO THE ESTIMATES?

The best people to undertake the estimates are the ones who are going to undertake the work. Clearly, they must have some relevant experience or they are going to have no baseline with which to compare the new project. Conversely, there can be no role for a "professional estimator" because the technical experience of such a person would soon become so out-of-date as to be worthless. I undertake many estimates, but I have to match that task with substantive project work, or else by now I would be mapping mainframe/dumb terminal assumptions onto server/browser applications.

So the ideal estimator is the project manager or technical manager who has been nominated for the work in hand. He or she may draw on specific experience from the proposed team—the developers who will actually be doing the work—but someone is needed to collate the results and take responsibility for the total. If there are projects with which this one can be validly compared, some expertise in the application area, or any familiarity with the technology to be used, the relevant people need to be brought into the estimation team or made available for consultation.

Where the professional estimator *is* useful is in the promotion of consistent technique. If everyone in your organisation has their own secret way of deriving estimates, and these are never questioned or the outcome validated, you will never get any better at sizing new projects. The methodology must be open, consistent, subject to challenge at a review, and calibrated at the end of each project. Someone needs to make sure that this is the case; in larger organisations this is a full-time role for someone within the software engineering function.

WHEN CAN AN ESTIMATE BE PROVIDED?

A few years ago, while I was working in a software house, I was passed in the corridor by a senior manager. "How long do you think it would take to do a C++ compiler?" he asked by way of greeting. I gave a number of person-years, and we passed without a further word. I don't know why he wanted this number, and probably never will. The point is that he probably didn't know if such a project would take one or one thousand years. He could have been on his way to a meeting where that lack of knowledge could have made both him and our company look so inept as to be unemployable. Many people would not have given that manager a straight answer to his query, and I can see why.

"What machine?", "Where?", "What version of C++?", and "What have we got to start with?" are just some of the questions I could have asked, and so wriggled out. But that was not an option; my manager wanted a number that minute. Not to have provided one would be estimidity in action. So we come to Rule 2.

> **Blindingly Obvious Rule of Estimation Number 2**
> *You can always provide an estimate.*

I don't care if there are hundreds of things about the project that you don't know (e.g., what it does, what the performance requirements are, what the platform is, what methodology you're using, what the language is, or what level of testing is needed), it is always possible to come up with some number, regardless of the number of caveats you may care to set with it.

Army privates have a saying that there is no greater danger than an officer with a map; I have that same feeling about managers and estimates. We all know that your number will be cast in stone, and the caveats will be forgotten. Such is life. You may argue that a figure plucked from the air has no validity—a guess is not an estimate. But my manager chose me to help with his problem because he knew that I had the experience to provide an estimate of sufficient accuracy for his purpose. To evade such a responsibility under a smokescreen of excuses would not help anyone.

WHERE DO YOU START?

Techniques for estimation fall into four categories:

1. **Expert Judgment**—Consult with one or more experts, who use their experience to arrive at an estimate.
2. **Analogy**—Compare the proposed project with one or more completed systems, analysing similarities and differences in order to derive the estimate.
3. **Bottom-Up**—Decompose the work into its components, estimate each of these individually, and then sum the results to obtain an overall figure.
4. **Algorithmic**—Use a mathematical model to derive the cost or timescale. Input parameters define the unique characteristics of the project, and these are fed into a set of equations in order to obtain an estimate.

Expert judgment is fine, so long as you can find an expert whom you trust. According to Delia Smith's *Complete Cookery Course*, it should take me three hours to make a steak-and-kidney pie. But does this mean I should start three hours before my dinner party begins, or should I be building in factors unique to my own situation—such as a lack of equipment, patience, and cooking ability? So choose your expert well, and don't accept his or her opinion unless it is directly applicable to your own environment and methods of working. That said, I would guess that the reason you are reading this book is that you are supposed to *be* one of the experts. Maybe you can get some specialist help, but you will also need some other techniques.

If I have made a chicken casserole several times before, I could conclude that it would take around the same time to cook my steak-and-kidney pie. Estimation by analogy is so psychologically appealing that it is tempting to see all kinds of previous projects as having some degree of commonality with the one proposed. But as the new project develops, the similarities fade away, and the task manifests unique and troublesome characteristics of its own. For my pie, I find that beef takes longer to cook than chicken, and making some pastry turns out to be more difficult than it looks. We may say, "The XYZ system took sixty person-years, and this one is pretty much the same, but with different technology, a less experienced team, and a new application area—so call it seventy person-years." But this is not going to be very accurate. It may do for a first pass, but could you then go on to detail all the differences and estimate these individually in order to obtain more precision? This is not to say that previous experience should be ignored. The more precedents and analogies we can incorporate, the more accurate our estimate will be; later in this book I show how this knowledge can be most effectively leveraged. But such expertise is better applied at a lower level rather than to the estimate as a whole. Estimation by analogy is fine for order-of-magnitude assessments, but only in cases where the projects really are directly comparable.

That's all I want to say about the first two categories of estimation technique; the remainder of this book concentrates on the bottom-up and algorithmic methods. But the best approach is a combination of all four. Assemble the most experienced team you can, employ analogies to get a feel for the overall problem, use the bottom-up technique to increase the accuracy, and deploy algorithmic tools if you think they will help to confirm the result. Above all, don't try to economise by using unqualified people, allowing insufficient time, prejudging the result, or failing to build on your previous experience. The penalties of inaccurate estimation are so high that it is worth an investment to get the best result possible.

What Is Contingency?

The Dilemma

How long does it take you to get to work in the morning—from shutting your front door to settling down in your office chair? Very few of us could state a fixed time, say, forty-eight minutes. It *would* be forty-eight minutes if your car starts, if you don't forget your bus pass, if your train is on time, if you can find a space in the traffic to cross the road, and if you are not abducted by aliens from the planet Zog. So you could say it is "fifty-five minutes on average" or "usually somewhere between forty-eight and sixty-five minutes." In fact, there is no top limit; there are factors—**risks**—that could ensure that you never reached work at all.

Now suppose I asked you to give me an estimate of how long it will take you to get to work *next Monday*, and I will fine you a dollar for each minute you are out either way. Clearly, "forty-eight minutes" is not a good answer, for you have to take some account of the risks. On the other hand, you can't assume that *every* risk will occur, or you'll end up owing me a lot of money should you happen to arrive after forty-eight minutes. This is the dilemma of project estimation. Determining a minimum figure is hard enough, but we also need to make an allowance for the risks. If we make too little allowance then these hazards may be encountered and the project will be late, but if we add too much then it may not seem worthwhile to start the project at all.

So the existence of risk means that our estimate will always be uncertain. We cannot ignore this uncertainty, but must embrace it within the estimation and planning process. This is Rule 3.

> **Blindingly Obvious Rule of Estimation Number 3**
> *Every estimate must have a contingency allowance.*

An estimate consists of two figures, the **base** and the **contingency**. They are as inseparable as the x and y values in a pair of coordinates. The contingency is an estimate in itself, of the amount of trust that that you are placing in the base value. This is not the same as a degree of tolerance, the way a 100-Ω resistor may be ± 1 percent. The resistor may be 99-Ω, but a task estimated at twenty days with 50 percent contingency is never going to take ten days. What that pair of figures says is that the task will take at least twenty days, and the best allowance to make is thirty days.

Separating Risk from the Base Value

Some people have more risky journeys to work than others. If you live nearby and walk in, your estimate for next Monday may be ten minutes plus two minutes' contingency. Or you may take several trains and be highly dependent on whether you make the connections—maybe forty-five minutes plus thirty minutes' contingency. Similarly, some projects are more risky than others. We may have undertaken a similar development many times before and therefore have a procedure for pretty much everything that could happen. Or we may be venturing into the unknown, not really understanding either the problem or the solution. The point is that the risk is reflected *only* in the contingency, not the base value. The latter reflects how long we think things will take if everything goes well, and the contingency is the allowance we will make for the untoward.

Separating the base value from the contingency actually makes the estimation process easier. It's still hard, mind you, but it does mean that we can determine our base value without needing to take account of all the bad things that may happen, and also that we can use some risk analysis techniques to determine the right level of contingency.

The Sweet Spot

That "right level" is dependent on the amount of risk you wish to take. Remember that the estimate is a statistical value—a point on the bell curve of possible

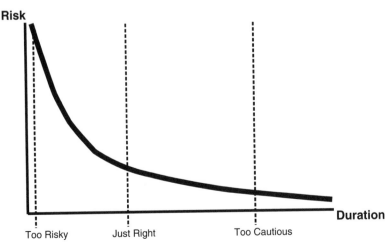

FIGURE 1.3. Estimates Incorporating Differing Levels of Risk

task durations. As Figure 1.3 shows, you *could* set your estimate as the minimum time the task could possibly take. That would be very risky. Alternatively, you could make an aggressive estimate hoping that not too many risks occur, or a "safe" estimate, allowing more time. But the estimate is never going to be completely safe because there are always more risks that could ensure that the task never finishes.

What you are looking for is the "sweet spot" that allows enough contingency to relieve your estimidity but not so much that the figures become ridiculously pessimistic. I discuss how to determine this point, and how to avoid excessive caution, later.

In a commercial environment, contingency is often seen as some potential additional profit. It is not. It is money you expect to spend, although the probability of doing so is less than 100 percent, and you don't know exactly where or when it will be used. You may be lucky—but don't bank on it.

CHAPTER 2

Listing the Tasks

The mightiest rivers lose their force when split into several streams.
—*Ovid*

MY SECRET METHOD

A great deal has been written about estimation methodology, some of which is so complex and abstracted as to be impossible to apply to any real-life situation. But so as not to be left out, I have defined a methodology of my own:

1. Make a list of the things to be estimated.
2. Estimate each of them.
3. Add all the all the estimates together.
4. Add a contingency allowance.

Well, at least it has the virtue of simplicity. But it is not quite as unsubtle as it looks. Most techniques assume that Step 1 has already been accomplished and devote themselves to all sorts of fancy tricks in order to achieve Step 2. But it is Step 1 that's the tough one—which brings us to Rule 4.

> **Blindingly Obvious Rule of Estimation Number 4**
> *It is harder to make the list of the items to be*
> *estimated than it is to estimate each item.*

If you have undertaken several IT projects, you will know that it's the work which everybody forgets about that really screws things up. I'm not talking about predictable risks here, for they can be evaluated and some contingency made. I mean the items—they may be tasks or may be risks—that could have been foreseen, but which were somehow forgotten and never even made it into the estimate. For example, I once worked on a large project that implemented around 250 data entry screens to place orders, check stocks, produce manifests, and so on. Somewhere in the Functional Specification for this system, it mentioned that on-line context-sensitive help would be available to assist the users in their tasks. Unfortunately, this feature was forgotten when it came to undertake the estimates and, indeed, until some overenthusiastic testers tried the "Help" option. Writing 250 screens worth of context-sensitive help text made the project overrun by nearly three months.

So the hardest tasks when undertaking an estimate are to make one list of all the work to be done and another of all the possible risks. Your estimate will be rendered inaccurate not by the figures you place by each item on these lists, but by omissions from the lists themselves. I'm not saying that *everything* can be predicted in advance—unplanned additional work will still arise. But at least we can list all the tasks we know will be needed, and all the risks we can foresee at present, one of which will be that the lists are incomplete.

FAMILIARISATION WITH THE PROJECT

Step 1 of my secret method is to make a list of **estimatable entities**. These entities may include software, project management, technical management, hardware, licences, and third-party contributions—all the elements of the cost of the system.

In order to draw up this list, and to make sure nothing is left out, we will need to become very familiar with the proposed project. I know I said earlier that it is always possible to provide an estimate, but it is pretty obvious that if we don't know a great deal about the work proposed, then our estimate is not going to be very good. This is Rule 5.

> **Blindingly Obvious Rule of Estimation Number 5**
> *The quality of your estimate depends on your familiarity with the proposed project.*

Because I believe in estimating entirely by "feel" there is no shortcut here. I always want to know *everything* about the project: the history, the underlying business needs, our relationship with the customer or users, the person who wrote the functional specification, the stability of the requirements, the performance criteria, the name of the designated project manager—everything we have. The human brain works in a mysterious way. Think of the qualities that attract you to your friends—the circumstances under which you met, what was said, and how the relationship grew. You ended up with an accumulation of feelings gathered from innumerable disparate pieces of information. At the time, most of these elements seemed irrelevant, unrelated, or even irrational, but somehow they were synthesised to produce a "policy" by which a close friend could be distinguished from many mere acquaintances. Similarly, when you are undertaking your estimate, nothing is unimportant—it all contributes to your overall feel about the project.

So the first essential is to read and re-read every relevant document and to meet all the people who are involved. Ask questions, and so get to know what the project is *really* all about. You will only have a limited time in which to undertake your estimate, but at least half of this should be taken up with research and with the all-important space to allow your natural instincts for evaluation; abstraction; and, yes, estimation to get to work. You will need to make some decisions about which parts of your investigation will yield the greatest value, so don't get bogged down in one area—say, the technology or the functionality—when other factors may have more influence.

THE ESTIMATABLE ENTITIES

So let's assume you now have as good an understanding of the project as can be expected, given the time available, and you are thirsting to begin your estimate. You now need to consider Rule 6.

> **Blindingly Obvious Rule of Estimation Number 6**
> *The more bits it's in, the longer it gets.*

Breaking a project down into smaller subunits causes your estimate to increase in size. You are thinking about the tasks in more depth, so more potential problems emerge and more time needs to be allowed. And there is the "minimum size" factor whereby no task can take less than—what? one month? half a day?—so the final total is inflated. It was fortunate that I was not suffering from estimidity when I gave that estimate for a C++ compiler to my manager. Had I subsequently attempted a design, broken that down into routines, and then estimated all of those, I would have started to worry about what he had done with my original figure.

So whatever the stage in the project life cycle at which you undertake your estimate, you must attempt to decompose the overall task into some smaller, more estimatable chunks. Obviously, there is a limit to the level of decomposition, and this will depend on what you have to start with—you can't start listing individual code modules if all you have is a feasibility study. If the project is in the concept stage, and we are following a "waterfall" project life cycle, the list may include headings like these:

- Feasibility Study and/or Proof of Concept exercise
- Functional Specification
- Prototype
- Technical Specification
- Code and unit test each subsystem
- Integration Test Specification
- Integration test
- System Test Specification
- System test
- Acceptance Test Specification
- Acceptance test
- User documentation and packaging
- User training
- Internal training—support and sales
- Rollout Plan
- Rollout and integration with existing systems

- Post acceptance support
- Project management
- Technical support

If we are further into the life cycle, and the Functional Specification has been written, the code and unit test stages can be broken down further. And once the Technical Specification is complete, we can decompose the list to the level of individual software components. More bits, so a more accurate estimate. Obviously, we have to stop somewhere—we are not going to start estimating individual lines of code. You are looking for a level of decomposition appropriate to the information you have to hand and the time that is available to you. Also, the level of granularity should be about the same throughout—there is no point in estimating a hundred tiny tasks if they are going to be outweighed by a couple of huge ones.

Entries in the Task List are items of work, not roles or individuals. You may find it easier to think of possible project roles, as well as the technical tasks, in order to make sure the Task List is complete, but make sure you end up with a list of items to estimate, not a description of the organisational structure.

It may be possible to agree the list of estimatable entities with other team members, individuals who have accomplished similar projects in the past, or even your customer. People are usually far more willing to discuss the inventory of tasks than to undertake any other part of the estimation process.

TASKS EASILY FORGOTTEN

As I have said, omissions from the list of estimatable entities are more critical than the estimation of each one. Some that are regularly ignored include the following:

- business justification
- business process modelling
- familiarisation
- selection or design of project processes
- getting documents agreed with customers or users
- design and agreement of the user interface
- hardware (development and target systems)—selection, purchase, installation, and support

- systems software and development tools—selection, purchase, installation, and support
- setting up and understanding bought-in packages or "reused" modules
- bespoke code not directly attributable to any one function—things like:
  - common routines (e.g., for logging or stats collection)
  - interfaces to hardware
  - interfaces between components
  - testing/tracing tools, harnesses, simulators
  - system start-up/shutdown
  - backups, archiving
  - "programs" in SQL, macros, scripts, and so forth
- operator facilities to monitor and run the system
- help text on user screens, and other "ease of use" features
- "glue" code between bought-in packages or reused components
- system integration
- definition of test procedures and of the tests themselves, and maintenance of these definitions as development proceeds
- test data set-up and maintenance
- fallback and recovery procedures
- security features
- network design and testing
- testing that performance and sizing requirements have been met
- correcting problems found during testing
- moving from the development environment to the target or production system
- data take-on or conversion from existing systems
- business process implementation
- realisation of the benefits
- processing of change requests and the effect of these on the developers.
- walk-throughs and quality reviews
- the "project office"—technical management, secretarial support, team leaders, team coordination, system management, quality assurance, and so forth
- management of subcontractors
- technical documentation

Not all of these apply to every project, but the list shows that it is important to understand the scope of what you are estimating—it is easy to concentrate on the technical aspects instead of evaluating the whole business life cycle. There is nothing wrong with placing items into the Task List that you later find to be irrelevant—at least they are accounted for, and if they get a zero estimate then no harm is done.

COMPONENT-BASED DEVELOPMENT AND REUSE

There is nothing in my secret method that prevents it from being applied to object-oriented applications. The major elements that will form your list of estimatable entities are still these:

- design, whatever the notations, methodologies, and tools
- coding, say in C++ or Java
- testing, from individual objects and methods through to larger units
- overheads of project management

Details will depend on the development methods and quality procedures you decide to adopt.

All component-based development should have an eye to reuse. You may be recycling objects from previous developments, and you could be looking to build new objects such that they can be reused in later systems. Sometimes it is easier to develop new objects specific to a particular application and then to form a follow-up project to make the most appropriate modules reusable. These considerations do not affect the list of tasks, but may affect the estimates.

When reusing existing objects, there may be tasks to familiarise the development team with these, to get the modules up and running in the new environment, to modify them, and to retest them. There is also an additional risk—that the reused code may prove to be inapplicable or that it will need unexpected modifications. I discuss these topics further in Chapter 5 ("Analysing the Risks").

PACKAGED SOFTWARE

Use of commercial off-the-shelf (COTS) components will significantly affect the list of tasks. Indeed, for many modern systems, little or no bespoke code is needed, and the problem becomes one of configuring, integrating, and interfacing the selected packages.

The business case for deploying COTS solutions is often complex. Suppliers are driven by market forces rather than the specific internal requirements of your application, so future versions of the product may no longer meet your needs. You will have to consider additional effort to cater for product upgrades and for implementing and maintaining the "glue" or wrapper modules that interface between different components.

Other typical tasks on the list of estimatable entities will include the installation of each COTS component; initial configuration; specific programs in 4GL, SQL, or other more specialised languages; defining and building interfaces between the packages; and specific configuration for all the tasks and workflows in the desired application. Testing, of end-user applications and of operational processes, is still a major element of such projects.

Examples in this book assume that systems are built from bespoke code elements. But COTS-based projects still need to be planned, staffed, de-risked, implemented, and priced. So the overall estimation process and the Cost Model described here are perfectly applicable to such systems, but the list of tasks will be very different.

ITERATIVE DEVELOPMENT METHODS

Projects planned as a series of short stages, within which software components are delivered early and often, are less risky and often more successful than long "waterfall" developments in which the whole system is specified and then designed, coded, and tested. In an iterative or incremental environment, the system is grown organically rather than delivered in one lump. Typically, a part of the application is selected, this is designed and built quickly, and then the aims of the next stage of the project are determined. These may be to develop the first component further, build more components, improve the quality, or even to adopt a completely different approach. Another variant is to build a prototype and then determine how this needs to be adapted or rebuilt, after demonstrating it to the end-users. Alternatively, a "timeboxing" approach may be adopted in which the team sees how much can be achieved within a given time period and then re-plans, setting some aims for the next period. Such iterative processes are particularly suitable when the requirements are vague, the business environment is changing, or where the technical tools or techniques are unfamiliar to the project team.

It is tempting to imagine that we'd need to estimate only the first stage and could then look at the resources needed for the next once it has been completed. Unfortunately, the adoption of an iterative development life cycle does not necessarily mean that we can dispense with an assessment of the overall costs and benefits. Theory says that every stage will realise business benefits, so permitting a go/no-go decision to be taken or renewed at each iteration. In practice, however, the early iterations are often more concerned with creating the software environment—the baseline on which the later modules can be developed. There is no obvious business benefit from such stages, although they may well confirm that the chosen technological approach is sound, enabling the benefits to be realised later. But because we cannot always tie the progressive realisation of the benefits to the completion of each iteration of the development, any manager worth their salt will want some proof that it is worth starting the project at all and demand a timetable for when the benefits will begin to flow.

So the estimation process needs to reflect the iterative nature of the development more closely. Typically, we can envisage the next phase of the work—its aims, tasks, and risks—quite clearly, while the remainder will remain a little vague until that phase is complete. Hence the Task List should concentrate on this next stage, leaving the rest in a sketchy but still estimatable form. We don't necessarily know what all the other stages will involve, let alone how long they will take, but we can try to make an educated guess, revising this at the end

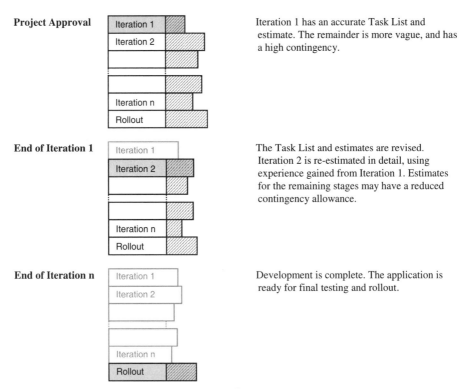

FIGURE 2.1. Estimation of Iterative Developments

of each iteration. For the first, or next, stage we can specify the tasks in more detail, costing that stage accurately as well as estimating the cost of the project as a whole. There will be a contingency allowance on both costs, which should gradually reduce as the project develops and the risks diminish.

It is always essential to keep the estimates up to date as a project develops— this is the subject of a later chapter of this book. The iterative technique provides the ideal staging points at which a re-evaluation can be undertaken. We can use the experience gained from previous stages to update the list of tasks and the corresponding estimates, in particular those for the next iteration. And we can review the risks, adjusting our contingency allowance appropriately. Figure 2.1 summarises the process.

Ideally, you should take the most complex and risky slice of the project to implement as the first or next stage. This will give more assurance that the completed system will work, and allow the estimates to be calibrated as accurately as possible.

Finally, remember that the Task List for each iteration will include care and maintenance of stages previously implemented. As the project develops, there will be more and more "completed" code to maintain, which to some extent erodes the time gained by progressively reducing the contingency.

THE COST MODEL TEMPLATE

The Cost Model template included with this book is a Microsoft Excel workbook showing tasks, staff, capital costs, risks, and all the other elements of a comprehensive estimate. I have developed it over many years, and use it for proposed projects of all types and sizes. Of course, you don't have use my template, and I am sure that if you do employ it then you will adapt it to the characteristics of your own projects or organisational standards. However, in this book I use my template to demonstrate all the steps in the estimation process. Whatever tools you adopt, these steps are essential for full and accurate project costing.

For clarity in printing, the illustrations in this book are not screenshots of the template itself, which is fully described in a later chapter and which can be seen on the included CD. In these illustrations, shaded cells indicate calculated values, or items carried forward from other sheets in the model, while unshaded cells show items to be entered by the user.

The first sheet is the Header, shown in Figure 2.2. Fields on this sheet are described in Table 2.1.

```
┌─────────────────────────────────────────────────────────────────────────────┐
│  COST MODEL                                                                   │
│                                                                               │
│  Project Name        ┌──────────────────────────────────────────────────────┐│
│                      │Example Project                                       ││
│                      └──────────────────────────────────────────────────────┘│
│  Estimate Date       ┌──────────┐                                            │
│                      │13-Jul-02 │                                            │
│                      └──────────┘                                            │
│  Project Start Date  ┌──────────┐                                            │
│                      │01-Aug-02 │                                            │
│                      └──────────┘                                            │
│  Reference Number    ┌──────┐                                                │
│                      │X01   │                                                │
│                      └──────┘                                                │
│  Currency            ┌─────┐                                                 │
│                      │USD  │                                                 │
│                      └─────┘                                                 │
│  Days Per Month      ┌────┐                                                  │
│                      │19  │                                                  │
│                      └────┘                                                  │
│                                                                               │
│  Project Summary                                                              │
│  ┌──────────────────────────────────────────────────────────────────────────┐│
│  │A very simple example designed to show how the Cost Model template is used.││
│  │                                                                          ││
│  └──────────────────────────────────────────────────────────────────────────┘│
│                                                                               │
│  Signoff                                                                      │
│  Role                        Name                      Signature              │
│  ┌──────────────────────┬──────────────────────┬──────────────────────────┐  │
│  │                      │                      │                          │  │
│  ├──────────────────────┼──────────────────────┼──────────────────────────┤  │
│  │                      │                      │                          │  │
│  ├──────────────────────┼──────────────────────┼──────────────────────────┤  │
│  │                      │                      │                          │  │
│  ├──────────────────────┼──────────────────────┼──────────────────────────┤  │
│  │                      │                      │                          │  │
│  ├──────────────────────┼──────────────────────┼──────────────────────────┤  │
│  │                      │                      │                          │  │
│  └──────────────────────┴──────────────────────┴──────────────────────────┘  │
│                                                                               │
│  Copyright © Paul Coombs 2002          Template Version 4.4, 13 June 2002      │
└─────────────────────────────────────────────────────────────────────────────┘
```

FIGURE 2.2. Cost Model Header Sheet

TABLE 2.1. Header Sheet Fields

Project Name	This should describe the project phase, subsystem, or option if there are several estimate workbooks for this project.
Estimate Date	This is filled in automatically and will distinguish between different versions of the estimate.
Project Start Date	This is used by some other sheets in the model to give month-by-month breakdowns of effort and cost.
Reference Number	Your own quotation number or proposal number, if relevant.
Currency	A three-letter code, such as USD or GBP, to indicate the currency being used for the estimate.
Days Per Month	The number of working days in a month, taking account of holidays, illness, and company overheads—typically 18 to 20.
Project Summary	An expansion of the "Project Name" giving more detail of what the estimate covers.
Signoff	The names of the estimators, reviewers, and those approving the estimate. This area can be altered in accordance with the sign-off procedures in your organisation.

Ref	Task	Notes
A	**Code and Unit Test**	
A1	Input Screens	
A2	Database Schemas	
A3	Reports	
A4	Usage Stats	Requirements vague
B	**Overheads**	
B1	Project Management	
B2	Specifications	
B3	Integration and Testing	

FIGURE 2.3. Task List

THE TASK LIST

The next sheet in the Cost Model is the Tasks sheet, which holds the list of tasks, with their estimates and contingency allowances, and also the plan for when each task will be implemented. For now we concentrate just on the list of tasks—an example of which is shown in Figure 2.3.

Of course, a real-life project has many more tasks, as is shown in the Case Study later in this book. But this simple example will serve to make the concepts clear, and I develop it throughout the next few chapters.

For the example, I am assuming that the production of bespoke code is the primary aim, although, as I have said, this will not be the case in all situations. You should insert the elements that will make up the main set of tasks for your particular project. Typically, you can distinguish between the **technical tasks**, in this case "Code and Unit Test" (Section A), and the **overhead tasks** of project management, testing, and documentation (Section B). Again, this particular distinction cannot always be made, or it may be too coarse a division, but you should be looking for alternative ways in which the Task List can be divided up into subsections.

TABLE 2.2. Tasks Sheet Columns

Reference	A cross-reference to the requirements document or whatever else you are working from. If there is no suitable reference system, make up your own.
Task	A brief description of the estimatable entity.
Notes	Remarks, usually about how the estimate was made or any reasons why the estimate or the contingency allowance is unusually high or low.

Table 2.2 shows the function of the columns in the Tasks sheet that I have illustrated so far.

So at this first stage of the estimation process, you should make your list of tasks and enter it into the Cost Model. You will almost certainly add more tasks during later stages—indeed the process is one of constant feedback and review of the model until you are satisfied all the sections are consistent and complete. The next stage is to undertake the estimate for each task, and in the following chapter I describe some of the possible techniques.

CHAPTER 3

Estimating Each Task

Nothing is so useless as a general maxim.
—*Lord Macaulay*

COMPONENTS OF A TECHNICAL TASK

We will now turn to evaluation of the base estimate for each task in the list. Usually, we will want to estimate the technical tasks first. This will allow us to estimate the overhead tasks either on a *pro rata* basis or as individual items once we have roughed out a project plan.

Whatever the estimation method, you need to understand what exactly is implied by a technical task within the development method you are using. For example, in a highly quality-conscious organisation a programmer may be required to adhere to the following process:

- Understand the function of, and interfaces to, the code unit, using some sort of Technical Specification—maybe with help from a team leader.
- Write the code, and get it to compile and integrate with relevant supporting routines.
- Write a Unit Test Specification.
- Write the test harness needed to undertake the unit test, integrating this with the module under test.

- Submit the code for review and undertake any changes required.
- Submit the Unit Test Specification for approval and undertake any changes required.
- Undertake the unit test, correcting faults that arise and retesting as needed.
- Submit the completed module for higher-level testing.

This may seem a lot, and you will have to use your judgment as to what you expect to happen in practice in your organisation. Remember that a day is quite a long time and that some of these sub-processes may take only a few minutes.

On the other hand, it is clear from looking at this list that the writing of code is a relatively small part of any technical task. There is a big difference between hacking out a quick Javascript demonstration and developing high-quality, production-ready, tested, supportable, and reusable software modules. Remember this when you estimate how long each function will take and also when people question why the estimate is so high for a routine that would "only take me a few minutes."

COLLATING YOUR ASSUMPTIONS

Whatever method you use, as you put your estimate by the side of each technical task you will undoubtedly have some worries, either specific to that task or applicable to the project as a whole. So we get to Rule 7.

> **Blindingly Obvious Rule of Estimation Number 7**
> *Write down your assumptions.*

Now this *is* tricky. It's the old problem about the mysterious workings of the brain again. Can we ever really know what subconscious assumptions we are making? But if we make a list of our assumptions then at least we have something to review, and then maybe our tortured subconscious will yield up the factors it is *really* worried about.

Assumptions fall into two groups: those that are specific to a single task, or set of tasks, and those that apply across the project. Typical task-specific assumptions may relate to how many fields there will be on the screen, how many records will be written to the database, or the complexity of the processing algorithms. Typical project-wide assumptions may concern the availability of resources, or the stability of the requirements.

In the Cost Model, task-specific assumptions are listed under the "Notes" column of the Tasks sheet, while the project-wide ones appear in the Risk Analysis. We are making two types of contingency allowance—one to cover task-level risks and then an additional allowance for project-wide risks. This may seem a lot, and I have often been accused of double-counting when people see my finished Cost Models, but the fact is that our estimate for each task has a risk factor, while the project as a whole is subject to additional, different risks.

Remember that the aim is to make you feel good about your estimates. One way to do that is to get some control over the elements you are worried about. But don't cheat by making generous allowances for a long list of assumptions you know are vague or unlikely. This is another manifestation of estimidity. I don't want to see an assumption like "staff have the appropriate technical skills" in your list if you already know who is to be in the team. Nor should there be a contingency allowance for "system capacity upgrades to meet the performance requirements" in cases where there is little chance of a problem. Contingency is not a euphemism for padding of the estimates—it is an honest appraisal and allowance for the risks.

ESTIMATING THE TASK CONTINGENCY

You know that, all being well, a particular task would take you twenty days, max. But it's probably not going to be you and, anyway, what if ... ? what if ... ? what if ... ? In a reasonable world, some of these assumptions may work out for the worst, while others will just disappear. As we saw with the earlier example about how long it takes you to get to work, you can never allow for every possible situation or else the safety margin would be infinite. We don't want to take the gloomiest possible view, but allow for a considered amount of risk.

The contingency allowed for each task is a percentage added to the base value to give the amount you are prepared to quote. It takes into account the assumptions you have listed against that task. The more risky the task, which usually reflects the extent to which you understand it, the greater the percentage will be. This is Rule 8.

> **Blindingly Obvious Rule of Estimation Number 8**
> *The contingency allowance is proportional to the risk.*

Base Total	150	Days		
Task Contingency		28.0%	42	Days
Total with Task Contingency			192	
Project Contingency				
GRAND TOTAL				192

Ref	Task	Base Days	Task Cont. %	Task Cont. Days	Project Cont.	Notes
A	**Code and Unit Test**					
A1	Input Screens	60	12%	67	67	
A2	Database Schemas	20	30%	26	26	
A3	Reports	30	30%	39	39	
A4	Usage Stats	40	50%	60	60	Requirements vague
B	**Overheads**					
B1	Project Management					
B2	Specifications					
B3	Integration and Testing					

FIGURE 3.1. Tasks Sheet with Estimates

Figure 3.1 shows the Tasks sheet for the example I used earlier, with the base estimate and task-level contingency inserted for the "Code and Unit Test" tasks. Table 3.1 describes the use of the task estimate columns.

In the example, I have given "Usage Stats" a baseline estimate of forty days. But in the "Notes" column I recorded a worry, which is that the requirements are unclear. This leads to a task contingency allowance of 50 percent and a "with contingency" figure of sixty days. For now, sixty days is the estimate I am prepared to quote, although there is still some project-wide contingency yet to be added.

The value of 50 percent came from the same place as the base value of forty days—somewhere in my subconscious, based on my overall experience,

TABLE 3.1. Task Estimate Columns

Base Days	Your estimate for this task, taking no account of risks.
Task Contingency	The percentage contingency that you are allowing to account for risks applicable only to this task. The spreadsheet determines how many days to add.
Project Contingency	The estimate (with task contingency) plus the contingency to be added to account for risks applicable to the project as a whole. This is covered in Chapter 5 ("Analysing the Risks").

combined with my in-depth study of the specific project being proposed. In this case, I reckoned that the requirements can't be *too* demanding and that I may be able to push back on anything too excessive. The other tasks have a smaller contingency, because I consider the risks against them as small, or—to put it another way—because I understand them better. Some areas always concern me—for example, external interfaces, itty-bitty details of screen behaviour, agreeing things with customers, acceptance testing, and support during initial live use. Other worries probably reflect my own skills, or lack of them—for example, communications is not my strongest area, so those tasks tend to get a generous contingency until someone can convince me that the problem is simpler than I imagine.

You will notice that *every* task has a contingency amount. In general, I will add 15 percent as an acknowledgement that the way I have derived the base figure is inherently inaccurate. You could argue that I should just add a little more into my base estimates, or assign 15 percent as a project-wide contingency, but I prefer to leave it visible and adjustable for each task. I may be persuaded to reduce this amount if, for example, there are some precedents or there are so many similar tasks that the risk really only applies to the first. Usually, however, I assume a 15 percent contingency before I have even begun to consider any specific risks. This strikes some people as an extraordinary amount—they expect the whole estimate to have an accuracy of around 10 percent. But remember that the "with contingency" figure is the one I am quoting, the one I am happy with, not a tolerance on some underlying "real" value.

On the other hand, I will rarely assign a task contingency of greater than 100 percent—indeed anything over 50 percent is uncommon for a project that has reached the Functional Specification stage. If we really can't say if a task will take, say, thirty days or ninety days, we must try to do more research to see if any of the risks can be eliminated. Or we may be able to cut out the high-risk tasks altogether and state, "this estimate does not include X, Y, and Z." But if that fails, and the contingency *has* to go over 100 percent then so be it—at least we can see the tasks that are going to be the troublemakers, and the reasons for that.

ESTIMATION TECHNIQUES

Ideally, our estimation methodology needs to give us a base value and a contingency allowance to cover the risks and assumptions. I have already given away my secret method—I just run down the list of estimatable entities and put a number of person-days and contingency by each one. I know there are more sophisticated techniques, but this brings us to Rule 9.

> ### Blindingly Obvious Rule of Estimation Number 9
> *There is no method that works.*

This is just another way of expressing Rule 1. If there *were* a foolproof method, we'd all be using it, every project would run to time, and this book would be unnecessary. So don't kid yourself into thinking that if you undertake your estimates in some pseudo-scientific way then the result is guaranteed to be accurate.

However, the point of this book is to make you feel good about the estimates you produce. So if you feel more comfortable following a formal methodology, or using a commercial product, that's fine, and I wouldn't oppose it. But I want to make sure you are not hiding behind the tool, claiming you have only turned the handle, and if the estimates turn out to be thickly sliced baloney with extra pickle then it's not your fault. It's still your estimate. If you don't have any idea what result is "about right" then I'd question whether you are qualified for the task—I'm not going to trust any method that is not backed up by a personal commitment. But if you do have such a view then why use the model or methodology of someone else?

Three fishermen had been waiting ten minutes for the fourth when he arrived, out of breath. "What kept you?" asked the three. "Well, it being Sunday morning it was a toss-up whether to come fishing or go to church." "So?" "I had to toss the coin thirty-three times before I got it right." As that fisherman knew, tossing a coin is a great way to make a decision, so long as you ask yourself if you are happy with the result. So what are you going to do if an estimation tool comes up with thirty days for a task you personally reckon would take ten days—or sixty? If you are using it as a check, a backup, or a reassurance then that's fine, but remember that the tool is a help, not a substitute. You must be happy with the result.

ESTIMATION BY FEEL

I have said that this is the method I usually adopt, but what factors influence my feel for the right base estimate for a task? I would pick the following as the most important and list them in roughly the following order:

- the size of the task
- the complexity of the task
- my familiarity with the task and the overall system within which it fits
- my familiarity with the technology we are using
- the skills and experience of the proposed team
- the amount of "process" that is being demanded
- special needs for speed, reliability, reusability, and so forth

As will be shown, there is a correlation between this list and the sort of factors used by estimation models like COCOMO. However, I would not like to state the relative weighting of one factor over another, which is highly dependent on the individual characteristics of the system being proposed.

ESTIMATION FROM A BASELINE TASK

I do not condone the commonly used method of dividing tasks into "easy", "medium", and "hard" and making the same estimate for each type. This is lazy and produces enormous inaccuracies. Typically, the "easy" tasks are overestimated, leading to lists of similar routines being allocated, say, three days each, when only the first will take this long. Alternatively, some really tough nuts are listed as "difficult" and woefully underestimated—some people think that *anything* can be done in a month. If you know enough about the tasks to classify them in this way then you know enough to give a more considered evaluation to each.

However, it is often the case that we can identify sets of coding tasks that are all roughly of the same type. For example, some of the functions might be classed as, "get some screen input, access some database records, do some calculations, put the result on the screen" or "get the report parameters, access the database, print the report lines, calculate and print the totals." If your estimatable entities can be grouped like this, you can select a typical task, spend some time in estimating this one, and then determine the rest *pro rata* according to their similarity to the baseline.

Let's take an example of a system that requires some transactions to enter data, plus some to produce management reports. For our baseline tasks, we can select the following:

- a typical transaction that calls for a couple of database entities to be read, a few lines of calculation, results to be displayed, screen input to be accepted and validated, and a couple of database entities to be written
- a typical report that needs a few database entities to be read, some calculation of totals, and finally some print formatting of the report lines

"A couple" and "a few lines"; I know it all sounds rather vague. But this is where your research pays off, for you are looking for baseline tasks applicable to *this particular project*. Maybe a typical transaction would call for one database entity to be read, maybe six. The average amount of "calculation" needed may be two lines of code, or may be ten pages. Perhaps your system is nothing like this—process control, for instance, where you are looking for a typical task in terms of the number of inputs and outputs, and the complexity of the interrelationships between these.

Now suppose we estimate our baseline task at ten days with a contingency of 25 percent. We might look at another task and think, "There's a few more fields on the screen, maybe a couple more entities to read from the database, but the same amount of calculation, so ... call it fifteen days. The algorithm for the calculation isn't specified, but it can't possibly be *too* complicated, so we'll push the contingency for this task to thirty-five percent."

In circumstances where there are many similar tasks, there is the possibility of making a spreadsheet of all the factors that influence the time they will take to complete, such as the one in Figure 3.2. Here, I have a number of reports that differ in the number of database entities that will need to be read, the complexity of any calculations, and the amount of output formatting needed. I assessed these factors for each report, and having estimated my baseline task—the "Sales Report"—I judged the remainder *pro rata*. Such a sheet can be inserted into the Cost Model workbook, carrying the totals forward to the main Tasks sheet.

This technique approaches the principles of Function Point Analysis, albeit in a rather do-it-yourself fashion. I explore this do-it-yourself technique further, after we have examined the more formal methodologies.

Ref	Task	Input Entities	Calculations	Output Formatting	Base Days	T Cont	Days	Notes
2.11	Sales Report	6	Medium	Easy	10	15%	12	Baseline for Report estimates
2.12	Inventory Report	3	Low	Easy	5	15%	6	
2.13	Sales by Area	6	Medium	Easy	10	15%	12	
2.14	Sales by Agent	12	Medium	Medium	20	15%	23	
2.15	Inventory by Model	12	Lots	Complex	30	15%	35	
2.16	Agent Expenses	12	Medium	Easy	20	15%	23	

FIGURE 3.2. Estimation from a Baseline Task

FUNCTION POINT ANALYSIS

Function Points provide an abstract measurement of the size and complexity of each software module and hence for the entire proposed system. Using precedents from previous projects (internal, publicly published, or commercially available), we can extrapolate how long the system will take to implement or at least determine the number of lines of code that will need to be written.

In this book, I provide just an outline of the method, so you can see if you think it can be usefully applied in your environment. For further details, see Chapter 12 ("References and Resources").

Calculating Unadjusted Function Points

To count the number of Function Points in a module, you must determine the following five factors:

1. **External Inputs**. Assessed as the number of "File Types" (i.e., data structures) and "Data Elements" (the average number of components in each "File") that are input as parameters to the module.
2. **External Outputs**. The output parameters, assessed as for "External Inputs."
3. **External Enquiries**. The number of transactions within the module where an input causes an immediate output.
4. **Internal Logical Files**. Assessed as the number of "Record Elements" (i.e., data structures) and "Data Elements" (the average number of components in each "Record") that are internal to the module
5. **External Interface Files**. The number of Record Elements and Data Elements set up by this module to be used by others, assessed as for "Internal Logical Files."

Each factor is assigned a value according to Table 3.2 in order to total the Unadjusted Function Points.

Calculating Adjusted Function Points

Armed with our count of Unadjusted Function Points, we now assess the following fourteen complexity factors:

1. Data sent via communications facilities (including terminals)
2. Distributed data or functions
3. Performance objectives

4. Usage of the operational configuration
5. Transaction rate
6. On-line data entry
7. End-user efficiency
8. On-line updates
9. Complex programming
10. Reusability
11. Ease of installation
12. Ease of operation
13. Multiple sites
14. Facilitation of change

TABLE 3.2. Function Point Factor Assessment

External Inputs	File Types	Data Elements		
		1–4	5–15	16+
	0–1	3	3	4
	2–3	3	4	6
	3+	4	6	6
External Outputs	File Types	Data Elements		
		1–5	6–19	20+
	0–1	4	4	5
	2–3	4	5	7
	3+	5	7	7
External Enquiries	File Types	Data Elements		
		1–5	6–19	20+
	0–1	3	3	4
	2–3	3	4	6
	3+	4	6	6
Internal Logical Files	Record Elements	Data Elements		
		1–19	20–50	51+
	1	7	7	10
	2–5	7	10	15
	6+	10	15	15
External Interface Files	Record Elements	Data Elements		
		1–19	20–50	51+
	1	5	5	7
	2–5	5	7	10
	6+	7	10	10

TABLE 3.3. Function Point Complexity Weightings	
Not applicable, or not influential	0
Insignificant influence	1
Moderate influence	2
Average influence	3
Significant influence	4
Strong influence	5

Each is given a weighting according to Table 3.3. We add these fourteen numbers to obtain the Programming Complexity (*PC*), converting the number of Unadjusted Function Points (*UFP*) to Adjusted Function Points (*AFP*) with the following formula:

$$AFP = UFP \times (0.65 + (0.01 \times PC)).$$

Converting to Lines of Code

There is no published model that links the number of Adjusted Function Points to a number of person-months for estimation purposes, although you could build one from your own experiences. However, you can attempt to convert the Function Points to a number of lines of code if you think that is meaningful and will help in the estimation process. Tables of multiplication factors have been derived from a so-called "backfiring" process, which involves assessing completed projects in terms of their Function Points and lines of code. The resulting factor depends on the programming language being employed and the table being used. For example, if you are using C++, one published table tells you to allow fifty-five lines of code per Function Point.

The idea of a "line of code" is itself rather hard to define. For example, should the count include comment lines? If not, then are we to assume that a thousand lines of uncommented code are as quick to produce as their fully commented equivalent? The Software Engineering Institute has produced a checklist to help define a "line of code" by deciding whether to include comments, declarations, auto-generated code, and so on. To find this, and the "backfiring" tables, see Chapter 12 ("References and Resources").

But never forget a final sanity check. Once you have determined the number of lines of code, ask yourself how many *pages* this would be (with headings, comments, and so on). Imagine this pile of listings on the table. Do you really think the whole project can be done with this much code? Do you really think it will take as much as this pile?

Variants of Function Points

A number of variants to the "Mark I" Function Point definition, as described earlier, have appeared, attempting to update it from its roots in serial files and batch programming. The best known are described below—further details can be found in Chapter 12 ("References and Resources").

- **Mark II Function Points** encompass the number of transactions as well as the amount of data. For each transaction, you add up the number of input data elements (I), the number of output data elements (O) and the number of data model entities accessed (D). The Mark II Function Points are then calculated as follows:

$$(0.58 \times I) + (0.26 \times O) + (1.66 \times D).$$

  Six additional complexity factors are used to derive Adjusted Function Points. Mark II Function Point Analysis has been utilised in the United Kingdom, especially for government projects, but has not been widely adopted elsewhere.

- **The Bang Metric** separates data-centric applications from function-centric applications. It considers functional and modified functional primitives; input, output, and stored data elements; states and transitions in a state transition model; entities and relationships between entities; and data relationships and data tokens. The metric achieves a higher precision at the cost of additional counting effort.

- **Feature Points** improve applicability to systems with a significant amount of internal processing (e.g., operating systems and communications systems) and so account for functions that are essential but invisible to the user. The method adds a new factor—algorithms—to the five used for Mark I Function Points.

- **Object Points** are generated by counting the number of screens, reports, and third-generation language components that will be involved in the application. Each element is categorised as "simple", "medium", or "difficult", and a multiplier is applied to each component. Object Points (renamed as Application Points) are emerging as an alternative to code size as the primary input to COCOMO in cases where that measure is inappropriate (e.g., where CASE tools are used to generate applications).

- **Cosmic Full Function Points** are a new-generation metric, initially aimed at business systems and real-time software. It is claimed that they draw the best from all existing measures, without being constrained by any of them. There is a *Measurement Manual* freely available on the Web, which may soon become an ISO standard.

Why Use Function Point Analysis?

The advantage of Function Point Analysis is that it provides a measure of complexity that is independent of programming language or type of project. Using data from previous projects, you could get an idea of your organisation's typical productivity in terms of Function Points per day. This would help in the estimation of new projects, as would comparisons with published information from industry studies. I don't believe that two projects each of 2,000 Function Points are necessarily going to take the same time to complete, but knowing that there *are* 2,000 Function Points provides a good basis for other factors to be applied. Whether the two projects will both end up with 110,000 lines of C++ is more contentious.

The main disadvantage of the technique is that you have to be well advanced within the development life cycle to be in a position to determine the number of Function Points. Design must have proceeded to the stage where the project has been broken down into functions, with each one analysed to the extent that such factors as the number of "Internal Logical Files" can be assessed. Estimates are usually needed way before this stage, so Function Point Analysis is no answer to a "shall we or shan't we" decision.

One of the drivers behind the development of Function Points was that the measure of "lines of code" is not directly related to system development time. Converting Function Points to lines of code rather seems to defeat the purpose, even it is necessary for use in COCOMO and similar models. There is a false impression that Function Points are non-subjective. Guesses and decisions are still needed, although these can be aided by the documentation of precedents and the imposition of standards. Finally, the Mark I method is based around mainframe technologies—"files", "inputs", and "outputs" are terms I threw out with my flowcharting template. While such elements may still underlie more modern concepts, the mapping is not always self-evident. Variants to the basic technique are not yet convincing, and don't much advance the cause of developing an objective method to determine a project's cost.

However, much work has been done in this field, and many organisations find Function Point Analysis of benefit—maybe not so much at the go/no-go stage but as projects become more mature and the designs firm up. If you can predict the number of function points in each subsystem as a part of the low-level design, you can check your progress against this, firstly by comparing the predicted point-count against the actual number for the first few modules and secondly by analysing your productivity in terms of the function points completed per day.

COCOMO

The Constructive Cost Model, COCOMO (now COCOMO II, issued in 1995), is an estimation model that takes a number of lines of code as input, and applies various cost drivers to yield the number of person-months it would take to implement them. Again, I will just provide an outline of the methodology, so you can evaluate if it would be useful to you—for further details see Chapter 12 ("References and Resources").

Basic Formulae

The amount of effort needed for a project is calculated using the following handy formula:

$$PM = A \times Size^E \times \prod_{i=1}^{n} EM_i$$

where PM is the total person-months of effort that will be needed (from the time the baseline requirements have been determined to the end of acceptance of the finished software); *EM* is one of the "Effort Multipliers" described later; and *Size* is expressed in thousands of lines of code. The latter can be derived from a Function Point Analysis (using the Unadjusted Function Points, because COCOMO contains its own complexity factors).

E is determined by another formula, as follows:

$$E = B + 0.01 \sum_{j=1}^{n} SF_j$$

where *SF* is one of the "Scale Factors" that I describe later.

A and *B* are factors that can be individually calibrated to reflect your own experience of the model. The two values *A* and *B* are needed because there is not a linear relationship between the number of lines of code and the effort needed to produce them. To take a simple example, if you find that COCOMO always predicts half the effort that your projects actually take, you can double the value of *A*.

Scale Factors and Effort Multipliers

The Scale Factors and Effort Multipliers reflect all the elements that affect how long it will take to develop some software of the stated *Size*. There is a long list of rules as to how to calculate each one of these, so Tables 3.4 and 3.5 just list what is measured.

A different set of Effort Multipliers applies in situations where the project is in its early design stages, and further models are available for development life cycles other than the traditional "waterfall", but I do not cover all those possibilities here.

To show how the factors and multipliers are evaluated and used, I take the "Programmer Capability" multiplier as an example. Here you must rate the communications, efficiency, and thoroughness of the development team with respect to what you consider the overall industry average. The multiplier can then be determined from Table 3.6. So if you have a particularly inept team, your project will take 35 percent longer than average, while a team of superstars will cut the development time by 25 percent.

As this example shows, the "nominal" value for the Effort Multipliers is 1.0; a lower rating increases the weighting and a higher rating decreases it. Conversely, the "best case" value for each of the Scale Factors is zero. For example, if the "Precentedness" is high, and the team have implemented this type of project

TABLE 3.4. COCOMO Scale Factors	
Precentedness	How similar this project is to others previously developed.
Development Flexibility	How much "room for manoeuvre" there is with the requirements; for instance, whether the project is trying to achieve some general goal such as a proof of concept or whether it is tightly constrained by contracts, timescales, or specifications.
Architecture/Risk Resolution	How much uncertainty there is on the architecture of the solution and whether a plan is in place to manage the risks.
Team Cohesion	How well the "stakeholders" in the project are working together. Stakeholders include users, customers, developers, maintainers, testers, suppliers, line management, and so on.
Process Maturity	How stringent and mature are the processes to be used during the development. The evaluation is based on the level achieved within the Software Engineering Institute's Capability Maturity Model (CMM).

a zillion times before, the value is zero; but as the Precentedness decreases its weighting increases, up to its maximum of 6.2.

Schedule Estimation

COCOMO also has a model for determining the elapsed time for the development. From this, we can see how large a team we would need. The formula is as follows:

$$TDEV = C \times PM^{(D + 0.2 \times (E - B))}$$

TABLE 3.5. COCOMO Effort Multipliers

Required Software Reliability	The extent to which failure of the software is critical—this can vary from a slight inconvenience to a threat to life.
Database Size	The effect of large test data requirements.
Product Complexity	The complexity of the code with respect to: • Control operations (straight-line code through to real-time control of multiple resources). • Computational operations (simple expressions through to sophisticated numerical analysis). • Device-dependent operations (simple read/writes through to performance-critical embedded systems). • Data management operations (standard database queries through to dynamic relational or object structures). • User interface management operations (simple forms through to multimedia or natural language).
Reusability	The need to produce modules that can be reused in future developments.
Documentation	The requirements for documentation at each stage in the life cycle.
Execution Time	The proportion of available processor resource that the system will utilise.
Storage	The proportion of available storage that the system will utilise.
Platform Volatility	The amount of change expected to underlying hardware or software platforms.
Analyst Capability	The skills and abilities of the people who will work on the architecture and design of the system.
Programmer Capability	The skills and abilities of the people who will develop and integrate the system.
Personnel Continuity	The amount of turnover among the people working on the project.
Applications Experience	The amount of experience the team has with this kind of application.

(continued)

TABLE 3.5 *(continued)*	
Platform Experience	The amount of experience the team has with the underlying hardware or software platforms for the system.
Language and Tool Experience	The amount of experience the team has with the programming languages and software tools to be used.
Use of Software Tools	The extent to which software tools will be used during the development, from simple editors and compilers to integrated whole-life-cycle development aids.
Multi-site Development	The effect of co-location or international distribution of the team, and the effectiveness of the communications channels between the different groups.
Required Development Schedule	The amount by which the required schedule differs from what would be considered a "normal" timeframe for this type of development.

where *TDEV* is the number of months the project will last—again from the time the baseline requirements have been determined to the end of acceptance of the finished software; *PM* is the total effort we determined earlier; *E* and *B* are the values we used to determine *PM*, which took into account all the Scale Factors; and *C* and *D* are factors by which you can tune this formula, as I discussed for the *A* and *B* values earlier.

TABLE 3.6. Evaluation of the Programmer Capability Multiplier

Capability	15th Percentile	35th Percentile	55th Percentile	75th Percentile	95th Percentile
Level	Very Low	Low	Nominal	High	Very High
Multiplier	1.35	1.15	1.00	0.88	0.75

Default Values

The default values for A and B are 2.94 and 0.91 respectively, so until you have built up some experience with the model, and can adjust it to your own circumstances, these will have to do. The sum of the "nominal" Scale Factors for a project average in all respects is 18.97, while the product of the Effort Multipliers for such a project is 1.0.

So if your project is perfectly "nominal" and consists of 100,000 lines of code then the equations yield:

$$E = 0.91 + (0.01 \times 18.97) = 1.0997$$
$$PM = 2.94 \times 100^{1.0997} \times 1 = 465.3.$$

Hence the development will take 465.3 person-months.

For schedule estimation, the default values for the tuning factors are $C = 3.67$, $D = 0.28$. So for our 100,000-line "nominal" project, the formula reduces to the following:

$$TDEV = 3.67 \times 465.3^{(0.28+0.2\times(1.0997-0.91))}.$$

This gives 25.87 months for the project duration. Dividing that into the total amount of effort yields a team size of around eighteen. The model does not take account of overhead roles, so if we added in a few more team members to cover these, the duration and team size seem well balanced (see "Blindingly Obvious Rule of Estimation Number 10", later in this book).

Variants of the Standard Model

There is a lot of research activity around COCOMO, both to refine and calibrate the basic model and to develop variants for modern development methods. The latter include the following:

* **COPSEMO** to align the model towards the project phases defined for the Rational Unified Process—inception, elaboration, construction, and transition.

* **Dynamic COCOMO** to acknowledge that some of the input parameters to the model change over time—for example, the learning curve as developers become familiar with the environment and application.

- **CORADMO** to apply to Rapid Application Development techniques—iteration, very high level languages, prototyping, and so on.

- **COCOTS** for systems partly or wholly built from commercial off-the-shelf (COTS) components.

- **COLQUALMO** to introduce a measure of quality (in terms of software defects) into the model.

- **COPROMO** to measure the cost-effectiveness of introducing new technologies or processes into a development organisation.

- **Expert COCOMO** to aid in identifying, quantifying, and managing project risks.

The adoption of Object Points (renamed Application Points) as a possible measure of "size" for input into COCOMO suggests that the basic model could be adapted for component-based and automated CASE applications.

These variants are mostly at early stages in their development, but show where research in heading. See Chapter 12 ("References and Resources") for relevant websites.

Why Use COCOMO?

There are many reasons I don't like, and indeed don't use, COCOMO. But it has the following plus points:

- It is easy to understand and to explain to management and customers.
- The model is in the public domain, which means it has been subject to an open process of comment, review, and validation.
- It can be calibrated to align with previous projects and with your own experience.
- The model will improve as the result of academic research and industry experience.
- Best of all, it is free, and there are some support tools available at no cost to enable you to enter and maintain your project details and see the estimates calculated by the model.

Its main disadvantage is its starting point. If we knew—*really* knew—how many lines of code we had to write then deriving a timescale and cost wouldn't seem too hard. But as with Function Point Analysis, we usually need to provide an estimate—often the most critical, decision-influencing estimate—well before we have undertaken the amount of design that would make this possible. And in any case, lines of code are not always a good measure of the effort needed to produce modern systems—integration and configuration of pre-packaged software may not result in all that much code, but still seem to take a great deal of time. If I were convinced of the validity of Function Points as a measure, and I believed that these could be converted to lines of code as an input to the model, then I'd be more confident. But as it is, I feel I'm multiplying a supposition by set of conjectures to get a result correct to four significant figures.

For even if you have a reasonable feel for the number of lines of code, you still have to make many guesses, often at things that are quite hard to assess. In which quartile is our programmer capability, for example? Even if I knew the names and skills of everyone who would be on the team (which is usually far from the case), I couldn't really tell you how they compared with the industry average. Most projects I've worked on have been staffed with a mixture of nincompoops and gurus, whose teamwork can shift from all-out war to near-psychic harmony within a single day. I'd have to call that "nominal." And are these lists of Scale Factors and Effort Multipliers really the *only* elements that will influence the time-frame for a development?

I have already made the point that an estimate is meaningless without its corresponding contingency allowance—our level of faith in the figure. COCOMO does not deal with risk, and I mistrust any method that returns one absolute value without a confidence level or any easy means of working one out. In my world-view, some of COCOMO's factors and multipliers *are* the risks—for instance, that I can't get the skills and experience for my project team that I have assumed in my base estimates. But I prefer to determine a contingency allowance specific to this project rather than to increase my estimate by some predetermined amount.

It is tempting to push all the factors and multipliers to the max under the principle, "COCOMO says it can't take longer than this, even if everything goes wrong." A very satisfactory situation all round—everybody thinks they've worked hard on the estimate and it's nobody's fault if the project never gets approved or if it all takes twice as long as predicted. We can blame the model for our estimidity.

Physicist Niels Bohr told a story about one of his neighbours, who fixed a horseshoe over the door to his house. A friend asked him, "Are you really superstitious? Do you honestly believe that this horseshoe will bring you luck?" He replied, "Of course not—but they say it works even if you don't believe in it." So even if you don't believe the numbers that COCOMO comes up with, it may provide some reassurance. And why not? That's what this book is all about: making you feel good about your own estimates. But I think you know the answer really, at least to the same accuracy you'll get after a great deal of effort with COCOMO.

COMMERCIALLY AVAILABLE TOOLS

There are plenty of products available—at a price—to assist in the estimation process. Some provide a vanilla implementation of COCOMO, including **COSTAR** and **ESTIMATE Professional**. Because the COCOMO model is in the public domain, you do at least know how such products go about their work. The models for the others listed below are trade secrets, so you need a certain amount of faith that your investment will be worthwhile.

Most of these products allow entry of the project parameters through a Windows interface and can produce plans, staff profiles, work breakdowns, and so on in a variety of tabular and graphical formats. For details of the vendors, see the Chapter 12 ("References and Resources").

- **SAGE** is based on the model developed by Dr. Randall Jensen at Hughes Aircraft Co. Originally, this only took account of technical elements (e.g., processes, tools, and languages) and some characteristics of the application being produced. However, comparison with actual project data revealed that these factors were by far outweighed by the effectiveness of the team. The latest version of SAGE gives a high weighting to the skills and experience of project mangers and their staff.

- **SLIM** was first developed in the early 1970s by Larry Putnam. The model is based on the assumption that the distribution of effort over the project life cycle follows the so-called Rayleigh Distribution, with the peak marking the end of development and the start of maintenance. The SLIM model is expressed as two equations, the Software Equation and the Manpower Buildup Equation, that relate software size, effort, schedule, productivity, and technology factors.

- **PRICE-S** is based on a model originally developed by RCA. It consists of three models: the Acquisition Model to forecast costs and schedules, the Sizing Model to estimate the size of the software (in lines of code or Function Points), and the Lifecycle Cost Model to incorporate maintenance and support phases within the development costs produced by the Acquisition Model. The product includes tools for risk assessment and "what if" analysis and is configurable for methodologies such as Rapid Application Development, prototyping, object orientation, code generation, and reuse.

- **ESTIMACS** was developed by Howard Rubin and is aimed primarily at management information systems. It focuses not just on the project at hand but also on how this will integrate into longer-term resource and risk strategies. Around twenty "Product Factors" influence five models, which are applied in turn: system development effort; staffing and cost; hardware configuration; risk; and "portfolio analysis", the strategic planning element.

- **SEER** is a mature model that incorporates all phases of the project life cycle, most types of application, and many development languages and methodologies. Inputs are an exhaustive list, including system size, personnel, environment, complexity, and constraints. Outputs include effort, cost, schedule, risk, maintenance, and reliability estimates. Its primary orientation is toward the support of military projects that adhere to Department of Defense standards, and it has a knowledge base of such systems.

- **KnowledgePlan** is based on studies by Capers Jones. It uses Function Points or lines of code as input and incorporates risk, quality, and reliability measures as well as the usual schedule and cost models. You can explore the cost/value implications of additional resources, more powerful languages, development tools, improved methods, and other technical changes. It even determines the impact of scope creep, showing how project schedule, cost, and quality will be affected by proposed changes.

- **CostXpert** combines several estimation techniques, including system dynamic modelling, knowledge based modelling, stochastic and deterministic modelling, and a variety of cost models (including the latest release of COCOMO). It is strong on the production of project plans, work breakdown structures, staffing profiles, and so on.

- **ObjectMetrix** was defined by a programme funded by the UK Government Department of Trade and Industry and the Scottish Industry Department. It is applicable to object oriented developments, incorporating the incremental methods and reuse associated with these. Elements of the project scope are collected and then apportioned across the defined range of development activities. The size and skills of the development team are also factors, alongside any special circumstances and risks. The result is not only a schedule but also a project cost. Estimates can be obtained early in the life cycle and refined at each iteration.

From time to time, I visit the greyhound track, where I am given a race-card showing the name, colour, age, owner, trainer, recent form, and a host of other details about each dog. It would be nice to think that there was a mathematical model within which all these factors could be combined in order to predict a winner for each race. Instead, all is chaos once the traps open and the hare is running. While it is clear, for example, that a good big dog will beat a good small dog most of the time, during any specific race the "historical" factors work together with random real-time factors to make the result unpredictable. But if we cannot create a model of an event with relatively few variables, like a greyhound race, what chance is there of an accurate and universal model for IT projects? Many of these commercial products look good, and their vendors claim great accuracy and a host of satisfied users. But I am sceptical of the underlying premise that projects *can* be modelled in this way, and I suspect that development methodologies will change too quickly to allow the models to keep up. So I'll save my money and restrict my gambling to the outsider in trap six.

Do-It-Yourself Function Point Analysis

Earlier, we looked at an example of a set of reports, estimated by assessing a number of factors with respect to a baseline task. See Figure 3.2 on page 36.

Looking more closely, there is some inconsistency in the way these estimates have been determined. Task 2.16 has twice the number of input entities than the baseline task, and this doubles the base estimate. Yet task 2.14 has twice the number of input entities *and* some more complex formatting, but again an estimate of double the baseline. Either I am assigning an inconsistent weighting to each factor or I am employing some additional judgment based on my understanding of the tasks in question. If I wanted to feel that I am applying some "science" to the estimate, neither of these explanations is satisfactory. It would be more methodological to list the full set of contributory factors and to apply a consistent weighting for each.

So we are approaching a combination of the techniques of estimation from a baseline task and the application of a COCOMO-like model. We can list all the factors that will affect how long it will take to implement a task of this type, assign a weighting to each, and use a spreadsheet to calculate all the estimates.

Some of the factors may directly influence the base estimate—in the example, the number of "Input Entities" has a direct effect on the development time. But other factors may influence the contingency. For example, we may have been supplied with the layout of some of the reports, while for others the format is unspecified, making the task riskier to estimate. We need to distinguish between these two types of factor and make sure each is applied to the correct element of the estimate.

The full method is described by the following steps:

1. Identify all the factors that will make any of the tasks more or less difficult than the baseline.
2. For each of these factors, decide if it affects the base estimate or the contingency.
3. For the "base" factors determine a weighting system such that the total equals 100.
4. For the "contingency" factors determine the percentage increase that will need to be added if the specified factor is applicable.
5. Construct a spreadsheet that shows the list of factors and the weighting assigned to each. The spreadsheet should calculate the following for each task:
   a. The total weighting for "base" factors.
   b. The base estimate, determined from this total weighting relative to the weighting and base estimate for the baseline task.
   c. The total weighting for "contingency" factors.
   d. The contingency, determined from this total weighting relative to the weighting and contingency allowance for the baseline task.
6. Assign a rating to each factor for each task and marvel as your estimates are produced automatically.

Let's try an example. We have to produce estimates for a set of screens that allow data to be entered, stored, retrieved, and calculated. I have decided that the factors that determine how long it will take to implement each screen are as follows:

A. Number of fields on the screen.
B. Number of these fields that allow user input.
C. Number of fields that need some calculation before data is stored for this transaction.
D. Amount of calculation that is needed when the user hits "Enter."
E. Complexity of the calculations.
F. Number of data entities that need to be read or written.
G. Number of lookup tables to be accessed.

Factor	A	B	C	D	E	F	G	H	I	J	K	L		Base Weight	Days	M	N	O	T Cont %	Days	Notes
Weight	10	5	5	5	12	20	1	15	10	1	10	6	100			15	7	5			
Ref Task																					
1.1 Query Order	35	2	0	10	10	4	2	10	10	3	10	10		762	15	0	0	0	15	17	Baseline task for Screen estimates
1.2 Enter Order	40	22	4	30	20	10	9	30	10	29	40	20		1579	31	0	1	0	22	38	
1.3 Amend Order	40	22	4	20	20	15	9	30	20	25	40	30		1679	33	0	1	0	22	40	
1.4 Delete Order	25	2	0	0	0	4	2	5	10	3	10	10		417	8	0	1	0	22	10	
1.5 Stock Query	22	4	1	10	10	8	4	20	20	4	10	10		879	17	1	1	2	47	25	
1.6 Daily Summary	90	0	0	0	0	18	15	20	5	0	0	10		1575	31	2	1	1	57	49	

FIGURE 3.3. Estimation Model for Screen Development

H. Amount of screen manipulation needed on hitting "Enter."

I. Complexity of navigation to/from this screen.

J. Number of error messages that may be issued.

K. Amount of validation or cross-checking.

L. Whether this function is going to be particularly difficult to test for some reason.

M. How well the algorithm for the calculations is known.

N. How well we understand which data entities will be involved.

O. How well we understand how this function integrates with the rest of the system.

Here, A to L are "base" factors and M to O are "contingency" factors. I have constructed the spreadsheet shown in Figure 3.3.

For each of the "base" factors, I assigned a set of weights that total 100. The "Query Order" function is my baseline, for which I have estimated fifteen days with 15 percent contingency. For every task, including the baseline, I assessed a rating for each factor—for instance, the "Query Order" function has thirty-five fields on the screen. Some of the factors cannot be rated in absolute terms, so I have assigned a value that seems in keeping with the others. For example, I gave "Query Order" a value of 10 for factor D ("Amount of calculation that is needed when the user hits 'Enter'"), which allowed the other tasks to be evaluated in relation to this.

The spreadsheet then calculates the total weight by multiplying each rating by the weighting for that factor and then summing the total. The base estimate for each task is then determined *pro rata* to the estimate for the baseline task. For example, the "Enter Order" function has a total weighting of 1,579, which we divide by the baseline weighting of 762, multiplying the result by the baseline estimate of 15 days to get our base estimate for "Enter Order" of 31 days, after rounding.

The contingency has been determined in a different way. The weights represent additional percentages to be added to the baseline contingency allowance.

A rating of zero means that the risk is low or irrelevant for that task and will not cause any addition to the 15 percent assigned to the baseline task. Conversely, I have given factor M ("How well the algorithm for the calculations is known") a high rating for the "Daily Summary" screen because I have no information about the calculations required. Hence, the risk is high and this is reflected in the assigned task contingency.

There are many other ways we could construct such a model. For instance, we could do without the baseline task and try to determine the base estimates directly from the factor weightings and ratings. Also, there's no particular need to make the weights total 100—I just find this easier. Whatever the algorithm, the sheet can be inserted into the Cost Model workbook, with the total being carried forward to the main Tasks sheet.

The main advantage of this method is that you can be sure that there is some consistency between the estimates for similar types of task—if you work entirely by "gut feel" there is always a risk that near-identical tasks will get widely different estimates. Also, there are more elements to consider for each task, so the estimate is likely to be more accurate, if for no other reason than the extra amount of thought you have applied. Finally, you can calibrate your model, adjusting it as more experience is gained. In the example, we can assess the accuracy of the overall estimate once we have implemented the "Query Order" function, for we will have seen how long this actually took to develop and the factors that influenced this.

Disadvantages of the method start with the fact that it takes a great deal longer. There is also no guarantee that the list of factors is complete or that the weightings are accurate. Some factors are subjective and hard to rate in relation to the others. Finally, there is a false impression that the method is "scientific" when it just consists of a series of guesses like any other.

I would say that this technique is useful only where there are, say, thirty or more similar functions of a particular type. The amount of time you allot to the selection of factors and weights should depend on the relative importance of these functions within the estimate and the accuracy to which you feel that meaningful ratings can be determined.

CHAPTER 4

Planning the Project

Hopfstader's Law states: "Everything takes longer than you think it will, even if you take Hopfstader's Law into account."

—*Douglas R. Hopfstadter*

How Long Will the Project Last?

I will now assume that by one means or another you have an estimate for each technical task, along with the appropriate task-level contingency. You can now calculate the total effort for the technical elements and, for longer projects, a subtotal for each major component.

It is a great help at this point to have some feel for the size of the team and the duration of the overall development, including the overheads of project management, team leading, technical design, and so on. However, we have something of a chicken-and-egg situation—for example, the amount of project management effort depends on how long the project will last, and the amount of team leadership is proportional to the number of sub-teams. So at this point, I use a rough rule of thumb: The total amount of effort that will be needed is **four times** the total for the technical tasks. Obviously, this differs widely according to the characteristics of each project, but it will help for now.

Regarding the duration of the project, we come to Rule 10.

Blindingly Obvious Rule of Estimation Number 10
The project duration in months must be greater than the average number on the team.

Suppose our estimated time for technical tasks is forty-five person-months. Using my rule of thumb, we multiply by four to get a total project effort of 180 months. To obey Rule 10, the minimum project duration will be fourteen months, with an average team size of thirteen. We couldn't have a thirty-person team for six months, or the rule would be broken.

Rule 10 can be depicted in the graph shown in Figure 4.1, where the project timescale in months, or the average team size, is equal to the square root of the total effort. For smaller projects (totalling thirty-six person-months or less), I've increased either the duration or the team size because it always seems to take a while to overcome the initial inertia.

Now, if we applied Rule 10 too strictly, large projects would never start. For example, a project estimated at 100 person-years would need a team size of around thirty-five for three years. I would argue that this is the optimal timeframe for such a development, but in the real world nobody is prepared to wait that long. So I will add a corollary to Rule 10: If a project can be divided into

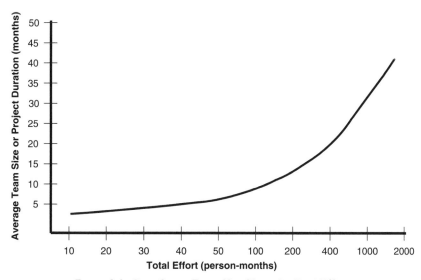

FIGURE **4.1. Duration or Team Size Given the Total Effort**

a number of independent subprojects then the rule can be applied individually to each of these. However, each subproject must be self-contained, with the minimum of dependencies on the others. There must be a "mother" project to draw them all together, with a central administrative office, and well-defined processes for integrating the deliverables from each subproject. All this must be reflected in the estimates, ideally with a separate Cost Model for each subproject and one for the mother project.

Most new developments ramp up to their maximum staffing level, because the team members drift in slowly from whatever else they have been doing and because the early tasks of detailed specification and design are not so demanding on resources. And the project will ramp down as the testing is completed and the later stages of rollout and support are reached. So you can't just take the square root of the total number of months and assume a team of that size will start on day one. A team with an average size of thirteen will start with just a few, say seven, rise to maybe twenty, and end with just one or two looking after the completed system. This is shown in Figure 4.2.

Maybe the end-date has already been determined—your customer has stated that the system must be up and running by a certain date. You can now compare the time available with the total effort estimates, calculate the number on the team, and see if Rule 10 is broken. If it is, don't panic yet; we are only using a few simple rules of thumb at this stage. However, you should begin to prepare for the possibility that the expectations can't be met.

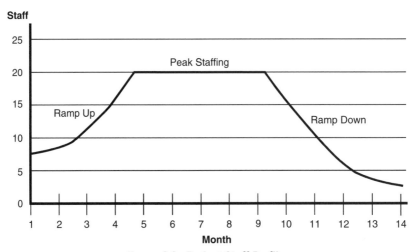

FIGURE 4.2. Project Staff Profile

On the other hand, the end-date may be up to you. We can now get a rough balance between the ideal project length and team size, given the total amount of work to be done. You may have some feeling for the maximum duration or the maximum team size that will be acceptable, so this could be the moment to share your initial thoughts with your superiors.

THE TASK PLAN

The next addition to our Cost Model is a preliminary Task Plan or Gantt Chart. You may be a fan of Microsoft Project or a similar package, but I prefer using the spreadsheet at this stage because it allows values to be imported from or exported to other parts of the Cost Model. Also, we will be revising this initial plan several times before we are through, so we need something simple and easy to change—we can draw up a more detailed schedule later.

For now, we will allocate time to tasks, not individual people, although we will be drawing one of those charts later. What we have right now is a guess at the overall duration of the project and estimates for a number of technical tasks. These tasks can be placed in the middle of the plan, as we know that we will have some other work to do, both before and after them. I mentioned earlier that my rule of thumb is that the total effort will be four times that estimated for the technical tasks. This breaks down as doubling the project length and then doubling the project depth (the number of people needed). So if our estimate for technical tasks is T, allow $\frac{1}{2}T$ before and $\frac{1}{2}T$ afterwards, as an initial assumption, although of course much depends on the individual characteristics of your project. You may have some other constraints, for instance, that some tasks have to be completed before others can be started, and these should be reflected in the plan. For my example project, the result is shown in Figure 4.3.

Ref	Task	Project Cont.	Check	Aug-02	Sep-02	Oct-02	Nov-02	Dec-02	Jan-03	Feb-03	Mar-03	Apr-03
			Staff Profile			3	3	3	2			
	GRAND TOTAL	192	209 Total			57	75	73	38			
A	**Code and Unit Test**											
A1	Input Screens	67	57				19	19	19			
A2	Database Schemas	26	38			38						
A3	Reports	39	38				19	19				
A4	Usage Stats	60	76			19	19	19	19			
B	**Overheads**											
B1	Project Management											
B2	Specifications											
B3	Integration and Testing											

FIGURE 4.3. Task Plan

In this case, you'll notice that the database schemas have to be finished before work on the input screens and reports can start. The figures entered are all multiples of 19, which is the number of days I am allowing per person per month.

To draw up this plan, I made a few assumptions about what the team size might be—two people for the database schemas and one each for screens, reports, and stats. The staff profile begins to look right, occupying half the chart and beginning to tail off. It fits with my rule of thumb for the size of the project: 192×4 is 768 days, or 40.4 months, so our average team size may be around six people for seven months. We have accounted for three or four of the team, and the overhead tasks will take care of the rest. I've allowed nine months in all for the project to ramp up and tail off.

The sheet shows a sanity check between the task estimates and the totals in the plan. As the plan is in months and the tasks are estimated in days, there is bound to be a disparity, but this should not be greater than 19, the number of working days in a month. Here we have totals of 192 and 209 days—similar enough at this stage.

Could there be other profiles? Supposing I doubled or tripled the team sizes for screens, reports, and stats, we would end up with a Task Plan such as that shown in Figure 4.4. Maybe the project could complete in four months, but our team size has already grown to seven before we have added any overhead tasks. If you think this is believable then that's fine—it's your estimate. I prefer to start with an even balance between team-size and duration and see how my customers or managers react. There will always be pressure to complete the project more quickly, and we are beginning to see that we will have the tools to demonstrate what this would imply.

Ref	Task	Project Cont.	Check	Aug-02	Sep-02	Oct-02	Nov-02	Dec-02	Jan-03	Feb-03	Mar-03	Apr-03
	Staff Profile				4	7						
	GRAND TOTAL	192	209 Total		76	133						
A	Code and Unit Test											
A1	Input Screens	67	57			57						
A2	Database Schemas	26	38		38							
A3	Reports	39	38			38						
A4	Usage Stats	60	76		38	38						
B	Overheads											
B1	Project Management											
B2	Specifications											
B3	Integration and Testing											

FIGURE 4.4. Alternative Task Plan

Task

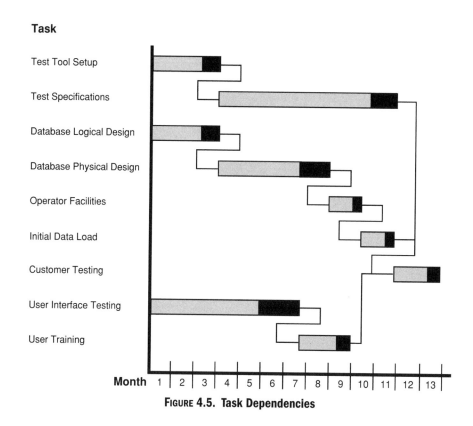

FIGURE 4.5. Task Dependencies

TASK AND RESOURCE DEPENDENCIES

In the example, I had to schedule the "Database Schemas" task before those for the "Input Screens" and "Reports" because the schemas have to be complete before we can start on the code modules that reference them. Understanding the dependencies between tasks is an essential part of the planning and estimation process. For more complex projects we will need to sketch out a dependency diagram such as Figure 4.5, where the dark shading shows the task-level contingency.

The Critical Path

Conventional project planning methods concentrate on the **Critical Path**, which is the longest chain of dependent tasks, as in Figure 4.6.

Task

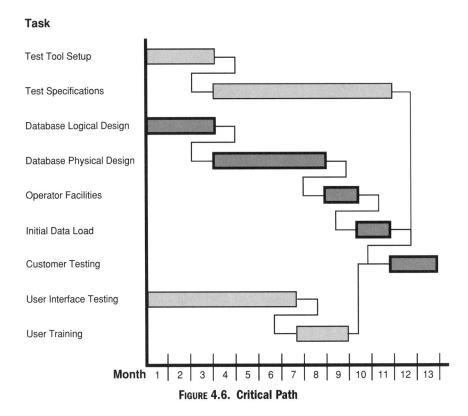

FIGURE 4.6. **Critical Path**

In his novel *Critical Chain*, Dr. Eliyahu Goldratt points out that such a plan takes no account of resource availability. As is shown later, this example schedule will turn out to be impossible.

Planning Backwards

Dr. Goldratt also points out that once we have determined a possible end-date (using Rule 10) we could plan backwards. Rather than scheduling each task to commence as soon as possible after the start date, we can plan for them to complete as late as possible towards the end date. This has advantages in that we don't incur staff costs any earlier than necessary and that we don't have too many tasks to manage from the moment the project commences. However, there is a snag—delays occur later in the schedule, reducing our flexibility to compensate or re-plan. I cover Goldratt's strategies for the allocation of contingency in Chapter 5 ("Analysing the Risks"), but for now we look at his methods for the planning of interdependent tasks.

Task

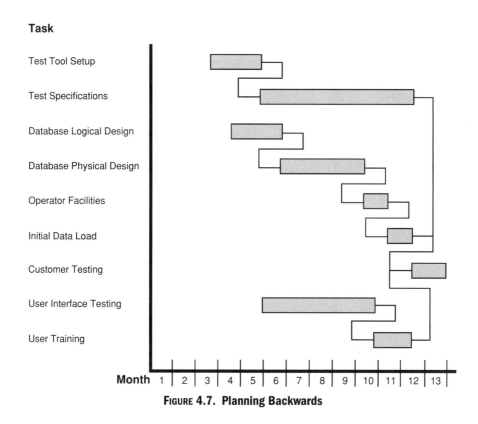

FIGURE **4.7. Planning Backwards**

In the example, we can remove the contingency and plan backwards from the given end-date of month 13, as shown by Figure 4.7.

Eliminating Resource Conflicts

As for any project, resources are limited—certain tasks can be undertaken only by specific team members. In this case, the situation is shown by the lettering in Figure 4.8.

Because of the skills mix on the team, person B must undertake the test specifications, customer testing, and user training. Similarly, the operator facilities and the user interface testing must be implemented by person C. However, our plan shows these people working on two tasks at once. We took no account of the resource dependencies, so the plan is just not feasible for this team, regardless of how much attention we pay to the critical path.

Task

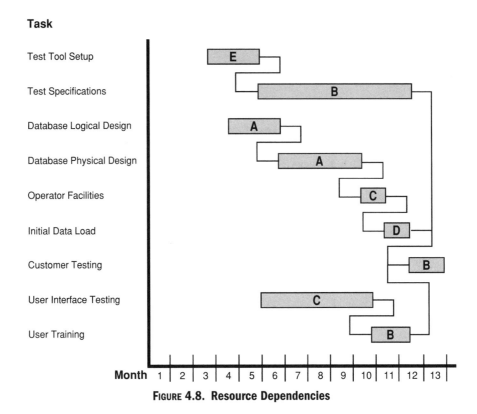

FIGURE **4.8. Resource Dependencies**

The schedule must be redrawn as in Figure 4.9, removing the resource con-flicts, while preserving the end-date if possible.

The Critical Chain

Goldratt defines the **Critical Chain** to be the longest chain of tasks, consider-ing the task dependencies *and* the resource dependencies. In Figure 4.10, the Critical Chain for the example project is outlined in bold.

As you can see, the Critical Chain may jump from path to path of dependent tasks. A good way to determine the Critical Chain is to imagine that you are pushing at the schedule from the right-hand edge. What is the set of tasks that prevents the timescale shortening, while preserving the dependencies and avoiding multitasking for project team members?

So in order to draw up the Task Plan, you need to consider the skills and experience of the project team, avoiding any resource conflicts. If the team

Task

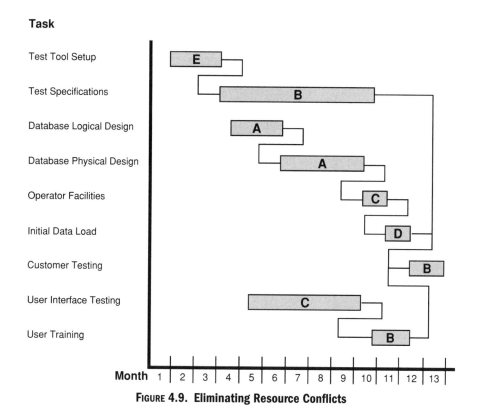

Test Tool Setup

Test Specifications

Database Logical Design

Database Physical Design

Operator Facilities

Initial Data Load

Customer Testing

User Interface Testing

User Training

Month 1 | 2 | 3 | 4 | 5 | 6 | 7 | 8 | 9 | 10 | 11 | 12 | 13 |

FIGURE 4.9. Eliminating Resource Conflicts

members are currently unknown then you can imagine that "ideal" people will fill each role, but you must monitor the actual team as each position is filled or else the Critical Chain may begin to extend beyond your envisaged end-date. I return to these ideas in later chapters.

OVERHEAD TASKS

Once we know roughly how long the project will last, we can turn to the non-technical or overhead tasks and see how they can be estimated. Typical overhead tasks are as follows:

- project set-up (e.g., development environment, accommodation, staff ramp-up, training, and familiarisation)
- project management
- technical management

Task

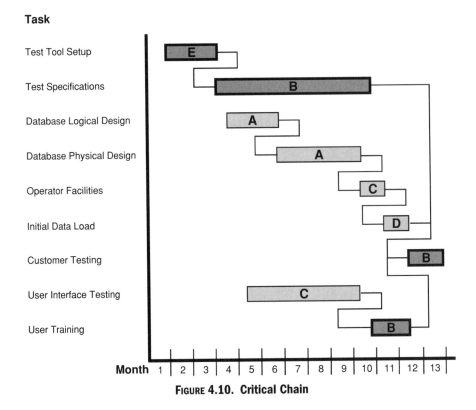

FIGURE 4.10. Critical Chain

- team leading
- team coordination
- support roles (e.g., project secretary and system management)
- system design
- writing documents and getting them agreed (e.g., specifications, plans, and user guides)
- feasibility studies or proof of concept exercises
- integration of completed code
- testing and fixing the bugs that are shown up by testing
- rollout, or cutting over to the new system (e.g., a period of parallel running)
- user training

It can be seen that some of these tasks, such as project management, are going to extend over the entire duration, or for a significant amount of it, so we can now enter an estimate for them. There will be no contingency unless you can think of any that is specific to the task itself. For example, the project manager will be needed for longer if the project overruns, but we will be including this possibility in our project-wide contingency allowance later.

Think about all the possible overhead project roles, choosing a mix appropriate to the particular requirements of this project. Deploying an extra person may significantly increase the cost. Conversely, forgetting that someone is needed can eat into the budget very quickly. As an example, I used to assign one junior person half-time to "system management" tasks, having a mental picture of daily backups and the occasional call to the hardware manufacturer's service engineers. However, applications now incorporate much more pre-packaged software—for example, databases, network management tools, communications packages, 4GL, and middleware. The system manager is responsible for the smooth operation of all this, which is a significant task, particularly at the start of the project. So my part-time person eventually became overwhelmed, and other members of the team were deployed to help, demolishing the estimated timescale and budget. Now I assign more, and more senior, people to this vital role.

Familiarisation

By "familiarisation" I mean the time for each team member to undertake the following tasks:

- Comprehend the project as a whole.
- Understand the part of the project for which they are responsible and how it relates to the rest.
- Find out about the project environment—how exactly do they compile a module and integrate it with the work of other team members?
- Learn to use any tools or methods with which they are unfamiliar—not just formal training, but actual hands-on use for this particular project.
- Become familiar with any packaged software that will make up their part of the system.

If these tasks are not allowed for, the project gets behind schedule within the first month. The British Computer Society review cited earlier found that 34.2 percent of managers never allow any learning time for staff on their projects. They seem to assume that suitably skilled staff will be instantly available or that the team can be sent on an all-encompassing training course before the project starts. And in commercial situations, customers may well ask why your organisation's project staff should be trained at their expense. So there is often pressure to remove the "familiarisation" overhead as an explicit task. If you cannot resist this, you must include as one of the risks the possibility that suitable staff will not be instantly productive. Some contingency can then be added which will cover the inevitable period while the team are coming to terms with their new assignment.

Project Management and Team Leading

Distribution of work between the project teams depends on the mix, size, and order of the tasks. You want the minimum number of dependencies between the different teams and well-defined interfaces between them. Each team-member will need a continual diet of work, so you should be looking for the points where transfers between teams can take place.

I allow for one person, full-time, to act as team leader for every six staff members. This rule can be adjusted according to the team sizes and the duration of their tasks. For example, if the team assigned to write the user documentation needs four people, you may allocate a team leader to them. But maybe that person can then be allotted some of the documentation work itself or be designated to manage another team of just two or three.

In a similar way, I allow for one project manager, or subproject manager, for every six team leaders. Of course, for smaller projects, where there's only a team of six or so, you don't need a project manger *and* a team leader.

Separate technical management is needed on larger projects. It is unfair to expect the project manager to assume the mantle of technical leader/designer/guru while coping with the day-to-day hassle of managing a large and unruly team. The skills needed are rarely found in the same person. Typically, a technical designer or architect will work with the project manager for most or all of the project's duration.

For even larger ventures, the "project office" may expand to include further roles. Maybe there will be a design and management team for each element of the system, plus secretarial support, a customer relations officer, a process team, a "keeper of the vision", a quality assurance team, a change request administrator, some external consultants, and more. The need for such overhead roles seems to grow exponentially as the size of the project increases, until it appears that only a few people are actually doing any real work. If you have a 100-person team, even with the appropriate number of team leaders, you are not going to run it successfully with just a couple of people at the centre.

Functional and Technical Specifications

It is reasonable to assume that the time taken for the production of specification documents is proportional to that estimated for the corresponding technical tasks. You can take a percentage of this time, according to your view of how difficult it is going to be to write each document and remembering that the result may need to be agreed with customers or users—a process that is often iterative and time consuming. To produce a Functional Specification I would start with a figure of 20 percent of the total effort needed for the technical tasks, and I would allow as much again for a Technical Specification. The Cost Model spreadsheet can then be used to calculate the estimate, so if you decide to alter the figures for the technical tasks, the time allowed for the specifications will be recalculated automatically.

In the case of technical specifications, there is often a long initial period of discussion, design, and walk-through before the details of each module can be documented, so it may be preferable to estimate this discussion time as a separate task.

Specification and design of a system are tasks with risks that need to be reflected in the associated task contingency. These risks are particularly high if the format and content of the documentation is predefined, leaving fewer possibilities to cut corners. But if this is not the case, and the content or quality of the design documentation may be sacrificed to meet the allotted timescale, there is an additional risk to the later implementation phases.

Testing

Testing is consistently underestimated—for two reasons:

1. There is a need to write and agree a Test Specification, a Test Plan, or both. Clearly, such documents need to be created before the testing begins—indeed, it is sometimes the case that acceptance tests are agreed at a very early stage, in accordance with the Functional Specification. The test specifications must then be kept in synch with changes to the system design, or changes to the functionality, that arise during the development. Otherwise, the testing is constantly stalled by disagreements between the testers and the developers as to what the modules being tested are actually supposed to do. However, the task of maintaining the test specifications is usually forgotten or ignored and time is wasted.

TABLE 4.1. Testing Time as a Proportion of Implementation	
Integration testing (of entire subsystems created from tested code modules)	30%
System testing (end-to-end for all subsystems together)	20%
Acceptance testing (to prove that the system meets the descriptions in its Functional Specification)	15%

2. An allowance must be made for fixes to the code that are needed following testing. If the tests are being conducted in parallel with the development, bug correction will disrupt the development team, who will need to return to modules they have probably forgotten all about and then find and fix the problems. Bugs found in the later stages of testing, which involve the exercise of many modules together, will often need cooperation between several members of the development team, and a considerable expense in person-days, before they can be fixed.

As, with the production of design specifications, it is reasonable to assume that testing is proportional to the amount of code; also, that it should decrease at each stage. Some starting figures, as a percentage of the time estimated for the corresponding technical tasks, are shown in Table 4.1.

Acceptance always takes longer than you think, because it is the first time that some of the customers or users have seen the finished system. This often leads to what might be termed a training session under the guise of disputes about functionality. Where this is a danger, it is prudent to allow for two phases—an internal "dry run" of the complete acceptance procedure in order to eliminate any problems and the actual test run with the customer. The base estimates and risks for each of these phases can then be evaluated separately.

REVISING THE MODEL

I'll assume now that you've completed your estimates of the overhead tasks and have some idea of the phases of the overall project and the order in which they will occur. Your Tasks sheet will look something like Figure 4.11.

Here I'm not too worried about the risks of the overhead tasks, so I've just applied my standard contingency of 15 percent. The plan now looks like Figure 4.12.

	Base Total	430	Days			
	Task Contingency	19.5%	84	Days		
	Total with Task Contingency		514			
	Project Contingency					
	GRAND TOTAL		514			

Ref	Task	Base Days	Task Cont. %	Task Cont. Days	Project Cont.	Notes
A	**Code and Unit Test**					
A1	Input Screens	60	12%	67	67	
A2	Database Schemas	20	30%	26	26	
A3	Reports	30	30%	39	39	
A4	Usage Stats	40	50%	60	60	Requirements vague
B	**Overheads**					
B1	Project Management	100	15%	115	115	
B2	Specifications	100	15%	115	115	
B3	Integration and Testing	80	15%	92	92	

FIGURE **4.11. Overhead Task Estimates**

The team profile is still looking reasonable, starting with four, peaking at five, and then ramping down to one part-time person to look after the on-site testing. The integration and testing task cannot get started until there is something to test, so does not begin until December. There is some intensive work at the beginning, to get the specifications written, but I feel this is acceptable for this particular project. Finally, the number of days from the task estimates and the Task Plan roughly agree—we'll get a chance to align these more closely at the next stage.

We are not finished yet, because the project-wide assumptions have to be factored in. Assessing the appropriate amount of contingency for these risks is the subject of the next chapter.

				Aug-02	Sep-02	Oct-02	Nov-02	Dec-02	Jan-03	Feb-03	Mar-03	Apr-03
			Staff Profile	4	4	4	4	5	4	1	0.5	0.5
	GRAND TOTAL	514	514 Total	76	76	76	76	95	76	19	10	10
Ref	Task	Project Cont.	Check									
A	**Code and Unit Test**											
A1	Input Screens	67	57					19	19	19		
A2	Database Schemas	26	38				38					
A3	Reports	39	38					19	19			
A4	Usage Stats	60	76				19	19	19	19		
B	**Overheads**											
B1	Project Management	115	114	19	19	19	19	19	19			
B2	Specifications	115	114	57	57							
B3	Integration and Testing	92	77					19	19	19	10	10

FIGURE **4.12. Task Plan with Overhead Tasks**

CHAPTER 5

Analysing the Risks

Being too cautious is the greatest risk of all.
—*Jawaharlal Nehru*

EVALUATING PROJECT-WIDE ASSUMPTIONS

Earlier, we identified our project-wide assumptions. We must now rephrase these as risks, and undertake a **Risk Analysis** to determine the correct amount of contingency to allow for them. This contingency may be estimated in terms of money, person-days, or a mixture of both. The Risk Analysis is another sheet in the Cost Model workbook—Table 5.1 shows the function of each field on the sheet. Figure 5.1 shows the Risk Analysis for the example project.

By making the Risk Analysis a part of the Cost Model workbook, we can carry forward some values from the individual task estimates. For Risk 1 in the example, I used the subtotal for "Input Screens" in the Task Plan as an element in the calculation of the "Maximum Days", so if I ever decided to change the estimate for the "Input Screens" task, it would automatically be reflected in a new contingency allowance. There is a "Scratchpad" area in the Cost Model workbook that allows such project-specific values to be calculated and named.

Some contingency allowances need to be calculated in terms of money, as I have shown for Risk 2. The procedure for determining the allowance for such risks is exactly the same as that for those determined in terms of days. Later

	TABLE 5.1. Risk Analysis Fields	
Section	Field	Description
Heading	Risk Number	A serial number to identify the risk.
Definition	Risk	A description of the risk to the project.
	Cause	The circumstances under which this risk could occur.
Management	Prevention	The steps that can be taken in advance to prevent the risk occurring.
	Trigger	The conditions under which the risk management plan will be instigated.
	Plan	The actions that will be taken to manage the risk if the trigger conditions occur.
	Owner	The person who is most responsible for ensuring that the risk does not occur and who will manage the problem if it does. This may be someone outside the project (e.g., a supplier).
Assessment	Probability	The probability of the risk occurring— estimated as low, medium, or high.
	Detection	The difficulty of detecting if the trigger condition has occurred or not— estimated as low, medium, or high.
	Impact	The impact on the project if the risk occurs— estimated as low, medium, or high.
	Overall	A percentage that will be used to weight the maximum possible impact of the risk. This is calculated automatically from the "Probability", "Detection", and "Impact" entries.
Contingency Allowance	Method	An explanation of the amount of work that will be needed and/or the costs that will be incurred if the risk occurs. This is the reasoning behind the entries for "Maximum Days" and "Maximum Cost."
	Maximum Days	The additional person-days that will be needed if the risk occurs.

(continued)

		TABLE 5.1 *(continued)*
Section	Field	Description
	Weighted Days	The additional days that will be needed if the risk occurs, weighted by (a) the probability of it occurring, (b) the probability of detecting it, and (c) its impact on the project. Calculated as "Maximum Days" times "Overall."
	Maximum Cost	The additional cost that will be incurred if the risk occurs. This cost does not include the time entered under "Maximum Days."
	Weighted Cost	The additional cost that will be incurred if the risk occurs, weighted by (a) the probability of it occurring, (b) the probability of detecting it, and (c) its relative impact on the project. Calculated as "Maximum Cost" times "Overall."

we will factor these money allowances in with the other capital costs that the project will incur. It is possible that some risks must be assessed in terms of a time element *and* a money element; this is permitted by the Cost Model.

ASSESSING EACH RISK

Whatever the terms in which a risk is assessed, you must be sure to include all the consequences should it occur. A useful technique is to have a look at all the project tasks and roles. For each risk, assess those that will be affected. Will this task take more time? Would its start time be postponed? Will this role be extended? Could a critical resource be delayed? Typical factors to consider for each risk are as follows:

- The extra technical work or time needed from technical staff
- More effort from team leaders to cover the extra technical work
- Additional testing time, quality assurance, and documentation for the extra technical work
- More time from the project manager and other support staff to cover the extended timeframe or additional effort
- Supplementary staff training, or the employment of contractors, to cover technical inexperience

| | Risks Estimated in Terms of Days | 79 |
| | Risks Estimated in Terms of Cost (USD) | 3929 |

RISK NUMBER 1

Definition

Risk	Technical problems during development of user interface
Cause	Assigned staff have little experience of ActiveX

Management

Prevention	Training course for 3 people (billed outside project). Some experience elsewhere on team.
Trigger	Development of ActiveX components deviating from plan. Team Leader feedback.
Plan	Find 2 experienced ActiveX developers to assist/train project team. Extend time to develop UI.
Owner	Dermot Trellis

Assessment

| Probability | L | Detection | M | Impact | H | Overall | 39% |

Contingency Allowance

Method	20% extra time to develop UI. 2 additional people over extended UI development time to assist/train proposed project team

| Maximum Days | 200 | | | **Weighted Days** | |
| Maximum Cost (USD) | | | | **Weighted Cost** | 79 |

RISK NUMBER 2

Definition

Risk	Client penalty clause
Cause	On-site testing not complete by end of September

Management

Prevention	Normal project management procedures. Current plan shows testing completed by end of July.
Trigger	In-house testing delayed beyond July.
Plan	Potential to increease manpower, but contingency is expressed in terms of the risk of the penalty clause bing invoked.
Owner	Ned Beaumont

Assessment

| Probability | L | Detection | M | Impact | M | Overall | 25% |

Contingency Allowance

Method	Fixed price penalty of $10,000

| Maximum Days | | | | **Weighted Days** | |
| Maximum Cost (USD) | 10000 | | | **Weighted Cost** | 3929 |

FIGURE 5.1. Example Project Risk Analysis

- Additional hardware to extend capacity, response times, and so on; this may entail extra installation and maintenance expenses

You must determine the *maximum* exposure—the grand total of all the days and costs that the risk may imply. Remember that this total will be weighted, so we are not including the entire risk exposure in the overall estimate. And you have to use some common sense. For example, it is possible that the entire team will be stricken with salmonella poisoning following the kick-off lunch, and thirty person-weeks will be lost. Even if you set all the assessment factors to "low", the Cost Model would still calculate a contingency of 16 days for this risk. But by a probability of "low" I don't mean *that* low. Risks should only be included in the analysis only if you feel that a contingency allowance needs to be made. Try to be more general—an allowance for the risk of key staff reporting sick, or otherwise becoming unavailable, is perfectly valid.

You might be starting to think that we are getting over-pessimistic with our allowances for contingency. We have already added some extra time for each task, and now we are piling on still more for the project-wide risks. But this seems fine to me, so long as we are not double-counting the same risk. Have another look at Risk 1 in the example. Here I have made an allowance for the team's lack of experience with ActiveX and applied a project-wide contingency allowance to the development of the User Interface (UI). But I may also have made a conscious or unconscious allowance for this risk when undertaking the task estimate for the UI code and test. This would be double-counting. Because I am making a project-wide allowance for this risk, the task estimate must be based on the assumption that people experienced with ActiveX will work on the UI.

COMMON RISKS

Some risks may apply to nearly all projects. Table 5.2 lists these, together with ways in which the maximum exposure may be determined. Many projects fail because of factors too general for this list, being more indicative of underlying organisational problems than attributable to a specific development. They include the following:

- unclear requirements or objectives
- unrealistic expectations of costs or timescales
- unstable business requirements
- lack of commitment from the project stakeholders
- poor communications between the stakeholders
- internal politics
- poor project management and planning skills
- roles and responsibilities not clear
- support arrangements not defined or ambiguous

No amount of contingency will ever compensate for these. If such problems exist, I strongly suggest you don't start any projects until you sort them out.

TABLE 5.2. Common Risks and Their Assessment

Risk	Exposure Calculation
A general underestimate because the estimation team is under-experienced, has been given insufficient time, or there are not many precedents or analogous projects with which this one can be compared. The list of tasks or the list of risks may be incomplete.	• Percentage addition to the base effort figure.
Requirements not sufficiently tied down.	• Time to assess proposed changes. • Time to implement unplanned changes and additions.
Insufficient experience or skills within the project team, especially for the top management or technical design positions, or where the team includes new staff, customer staff, or third-party staff.	• Training, external consultancy, or both. • Disruption to team.
Retention and availability of key team members throughout the project.	• Time taken to train replacements. • Disruption to team.
Communications problems because the development team is distributed over multiple sites.	• Time for meetings, conferences, walkthroughs, and so on. • Possible need for semi-permanent staff transfers.
Periods of slack time that may arise for some members of the team.	• Additional time, depending on the amount of interdependency between sub-teams.
Untried architectural solutions—especially if there has been no proof of concept exercise.	• Time to define a new solution, redesign, and undertake extra implementation work.
A development environment that does not reflect the reality of the operational situation.	• Time to migrate to the target environment, retest, and correct problems.
Inadequate, immature, or untried development processes, development environment, tools, external systems, or internally developed software.	• Training, external consultancy, or both. • Disruption to team.

(continued)

TABLE 5.2 *(continued)*	
Risk	Exposure Calculation
	• Time to redesign, implement, and retest internally developed software.
	• Time to re-architect and implement using different external software.
Ill-defined interfaces between system components, especially if these are being developed by customers, subcontractors, or other internal groups.	• Time to design, agree, implement, and test.
Re-used code proving inappropriate or hard to understand.	• Time to rewrite from scratch.
Dependencies on customers, subcontractors, or other internal projects.	• Possible idle time for team members.
	• Time for interfacing issues to be resolved.
Security, reliability, performance, or capacity issues, especially in cases where the actual figures cannot be predicted.	• Additional hardware and/or systems software.
	• Time to order, install, and test this.
	• Testing of the system under load.
	• Software changes and possible redesign.
Fluctuations in foreign currency exchange rates.	• Percentage allowance for affected items.

Unfortunately, the power to cure underlying organisational or relationship issues rarely lies with the humble estimator. However, the people who *can* knock some heads together, or kick the relevant butts, may be unaware of the problems. The estimator, who has undertaken the most research into the project as a whole, is probably in the best position to recommend the changes needed to the organisational environment so that success can be accomplished. These recommendations can accompany the estimate in a form that suggests that the estimated cost and timescale will only be achieved if certain issues are resolved. If the project is still approved without the problems being solved then at least you did what you could.

PENALTIES, DAMAGES, AND BONDS

In a commercial situation, there may be contract conditions under which you are obliged to make payments or refunds to your customer. These include the following:

- **Liquidated damages or penalties.** If you fail to meet a specified objective, you must pay the customer a sum in proportion to the extent to which you have failed. For example, you may be obliged to pay a certain amount for every month you are late. Or there may be a specified target for system performance (in terms of transactions per second, response time, or availability), and you will have to pay if you fall short of it.

- **Bonds.** An Advance Payment Bond is a guarantee that you will return all money paid at any time up to acceptance or the end of the warranty period. A Performance Bond is similar, but guarantees that you will pay a fixed sum (usually between 5 and 10 percent of the contract price). Bonds may be "on demand", where the customer can just claim payment, or "conditional" on some contracted requirement not being met.

However you try to limit the impact of such conditions, you will be left with a level of risk. This may be assessed as for any other, and the appropriate contingency allowance determined as an amount of money. For example, a bond can be assessed in terms of its value, the likelihood of the customer invoking it, the time at which it is called in, and the effect on the customer if you were to stop work or not deliver the system. Any increases to the contract price will in turn affect the value of the bond, so you will have to find some commercial balance between the contingency allowance and the price that you wish to quote.

It is possible to purchase insurance against unreasonable bond calls. For example, it is not unknown for customers to fail to create the organisational environment into which the project will be delivered, so then decide to call the bond. Or they may withhold payments, while threatening to call the bond if you stop work. You cannot cater for such risks by increasing the contract price, but you can lay them off elsewhere.

ALLOWANCES FOR POSITIVE FACTORS

We have been talking about adding project-wide contingency allowances to compensate for risks, but there may be some positive factors that would allow us to *reduce* our overall estimates. These include the following:

- reuse of existing code
- deployment of particularly skilled or experienced staff
- similarities between different parts of the system
- knowledge and expertise from other projects
- use of packaged solutions or development aids

Where such factors are undeniably advantageous (or the pressure to see them as such is irresistible), an allowance must be made. This should be assessed when drawing up the task-by-task estimates, not by applying some blanket rule such as "reduce the price by 25 percent to account for reuse of code from the XYZ system", because the positive factor may not apply to every element of the project. An extra column in the Tasks sheet will allow a specific assessment to be estimated and totalled.

Regarding reuse of existing modules, some rules of thumb are mentioned by Donald Reifer in his book *Making the Software Business Case: Improvement by the Numbers*:

- 20 percent of the code will be responsible for 80 percent of the reuse obtained.
- The additional cost to develop code for reuse is between 35 percent to 50 percent.
- The cost if code is reused is 20 percent to 25 percent of what it would be to develop everything from scratch.
- A module should not be developed for reuse unless there are three or more known uses for it.
- Reusable components will be ten times more reliable.
- Less than 10 percent of code meant to be throwaway is ever thrown away.

Another useful measure is the COCOMO formula to assess the relative importance of non-bespoke code. This is expressed as follows:

$$Software\ Size\ (Lines\ of\ Code) = New + 0.5(Modified)$$
$$+ 0.4(Reused) + 0.3(COTS).$$

For example, according to this formula, modifying one thousand lines of existing code takes half the time of writing those lines from scratch.

But will such factors reduce the project cost or not? It can take longer to understand and integrate existing code, however well it is documented, than to write the same modules from scratch. Customer staff may have some specific knowledge, but will the company cultures and processes meld or clash? Will two subsystems, which seem so similar now, actually turn out to be so in nine months' time? And will we actually get these so-called experts from that other project which is due to finish just as this one starts?

If I do adjust my estimates for such positive factors, I usually make an allowance for the reverse, as a project-wide risk. So I may remove ninety days from the code estimates because I am told that we can recycle some old code, but I will then add, say, thirty days contingency in case this code turns out to be useless. For if it is, we will waste time in finding out *and* we won't get the promised time saving. If the code is as reusable as they say, the project gains thirty days of spare time—which will probably be swallowed up by some other unforeseen circumstance in any case.

As an example, I once undertook an estimate for a project that proposed to employ a new 4GL development environment that was claimed to reduce development times by 70 percent. If I were able to quote only 30 percent of my current 3GL estimate for the project then the cost of the 4GL product seemed very attractive. However, looking at the life cycle for a typical technical task, I realised that the tool only helped with the coding, not the testing. There would be less code to test, but our project standards still demanded that test scripts be written and approved. Even if I accepted the claimed 70 percent reduction, I could only cut *my* code and unit test figures by 50 percent. And this reduction could not be applied to the later testing phases, because although there would be fewer lines of code, the amount of functionality to be tested would be unchanged. Furthermore, many of the other project tasks would be completely unaffected if the tool were used. I then added the extra task of training the team in the use of the product and assessed the additional risks—that the tool was unfamiliar and could prove unsuitable. Eventually, although there was a slight net reduction in the estimated effort, this was not outweighed by the purchase price of the 4GL environment. Of course, there could have been strategic factors that also needed to be taken into account—purchase of such tools may only be justified over several projects. However, this example demonstrates that wholesale reductions to completed estimates are rarely justified.

BUILDING THE CONTINGENCY INTO THE PLAN

So far, our plans contain the task-level contingency, but not the project-level contingency that we have just worked out. It would be possible to resolve this by slapping a fixed length of time on to the end, but there are a couple of reasons why this is not necessarily a good idea. Firstly, it does not look good when presenting the estimate to customers or managers—the contingency is usually a large amount and comes across as an artificial padding of the predicted timescale, however much you may argue. Secondly, it is not much use as a project plan—the contingency is not all consumed at the end, but in irregular lumps as the risks occur. The plan we want to present should be our best guess, with the contingency taken into account. There are two approaches we can take:

1. Increase all the task estimates by some percentage such that the new total number of days includes the entire project-wide contingency.
2. Include the contingency in discrete amounts—**buffers**—throughout the plan.

I look at these options in turn, but in between I discuss an important issue—where and why does the contingency allowance disappear?

INCREASING THE TASK ESTIMATES

This is a simple calculation, although we may not get it precise to the day, because of rounding. To return to my example project, the Task Estimation sheet now looks like Figure 5.2.

The Risk Analysis from Figure 5.1 showed up a total project contingency of seventy-nine days, and this has been automatically carried forward to the Tasks sheet. I manipulated the percentage figure to the left of this until I found that a value of 15.6 yielded an additional 79 days once the spreadsheet had added 15.6 percent to all the task figures, including the overheads.

Our task figures now include all of the contingency allowances other than the risk elements estimated in terms of money, which we will come to later. If I were asked how long it will take to code and test the "Reports" task, my answer would be forty-five days, because this includes an allowance for all the risks.

		Base Total	430	Days		
		Task Contingency	19.5%	84	Days	
		Total with Task Contingency		514		
		Project Contingency	15.60%	79	79	
		GRAND TOTAL			593	

Ref	Task	Base Days	Task Cont. %	Task Cont. Days	Project Cont.
A	**Code and Unit Test**				
A1	Input Screens	60	12%	67	77
A2	Database Schemas	20	30%	26	30
A3	Reports	30	30%	39	45
A4	Usage Stats	40	50%	60	69
B	**Overheads**				
B1	Project Management	100	15%	115	133
B2	Specifications	100	15%	115	133
B3	Integration and Testing	80	15%	92	106

FIGURE 5.2. Task Estimates with Project-Wide Contingency

Now you have some new task estimates, you have to go back to your plan, revising it to include the project-wide risks. Inevitably, this will push out the timeframe or increase the number of staff needed. For my example project, the revised plan looks like Figure 5.3.

Our staff profile still looks reasonable and the figures from the task estimates and the Task Plan tally pretty well. I'm not going to make them tally exactly, although I could do so by manipulating the figures in the Task Plan. Firstly, I don't believe the figures are *that* accurate—for example, it is somewhat unpredictable as to when staff will actually join and leave the project. Also, it is easier to draw up the Staff Plan if we think in multiples of the number of days in a month.

It might seem wrong to add some extra staff or lengthen the timescale just to cater for some contingency. For instance, could we deploy the extra staff only if they were needed? Well, yes. Remember I am trying to estimate the cost, not manage the project. It doesn't matter if the staff are allocated or held in reserve—I am going to include the contingency for them anyway. Day-to-day

					Aug-02	Sep-02	Oct-02	Nov-02	Dec-02	Jan-03	Feb-03	Mar-03	Apr-03
			Staff Profile		4	4	4.1	4.5	5	4.5	3.5	1	0.5
	GRAND TOTAL	593	592	Total	76	76	77	86	95	86	67	19	10
Ref	Task	Project Cont.	Check										
A	**Code and Unit Test**												
A1	Input Screens	77	76					19	19	19	19		
A2	Database Schemas	30	29				29						
A3	Reports	45	48					19	19	10			
A4	Usage Stats	69	67				10	19	19	19			
B	**Overheads**												
B1	Project Management	133	133		19	19	19	19	19	19	19		
B2	Specifications	133	133		57	57	19						
B3	Integration and Testing	106	106					10	19	19	29	19	10

FIGURE 5.3. Task Plan Incorporating Project-Wide Contingency

decisions as to when and how to deploy the effort estimated can then be made as the project develops. But that brings us to consider some better ways to allocate and manage our contingency allowances.

WHERE DOES THE CONTINGENCY DISAPPEAR?

I have already mentioned Dr. Eliyahu Goldratt's novel *Critical Chain*. In it, he makes a simple observation: Even when projects have a generous contingency allowance built into their schedule, they still finish late. Where or why does the contingency disappear? Dr. Goldratt has identified several causes: student syndrome, failure to capitalise on early completion, and multitasking. I discuss each in turn.

Student Syndrome

Figure 5.4 represents a task to develop a code module. We would allow a developer twenty days to code and test this routine. However, this is not an academic planning exercise. In real life, developers already have plenty on their "to do" list and are juggling priorities. They see that they have been given twenty days to accomplish a task that they think could be completed in fourteen. Other problems have a greater priority, so a start on this task is not made until day six—or later. But we added the contingency for a good reason—to allow for things to go wrong. If problems arise, there is no safety margin left, and the task is late. Goldratt calls this the **student syndrome** as a tribute to the masters of the art of procrastination.

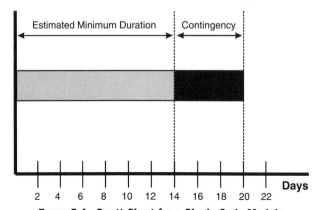

FIGURE **5.4. Gantt Chart for a Single Code Module**

Early Completion

Our estimate, with its contingency allowance, is only a guess, so, on the face of it, is as equally likely to be too high as too low. Despite this, it seems tasks are usually completed on time, or late, but never early. It is Parkinson's Law: The work expands to fit the time available. Should the developer complete the example code module on day 16, he or she may choose to undertake a little extra testing, make the solution more elegant, or just slack off for a day or two, knowing that his or her next task may not prove so easy. And there are other factors. If our developer was responsible for the original estimate and then announced that they had finished early, they may find their estimates for future tasks are shortened. It's safer to finish on time and get the praise for accurate estimation. I don't know how things are in your organisation, but I've never worked anywhere that offered much reward for early completion, but at plenty where there was a penalty for finishing late.

In any case, the developer may find the next task cannot be started immediately because it is dependent on other tasks that have not been fortunate enough to finish early. In the chart shown in Figure 5.5, task D depends on the completion of tasks A, B, and C. If C is completed in twelve days, but A or B

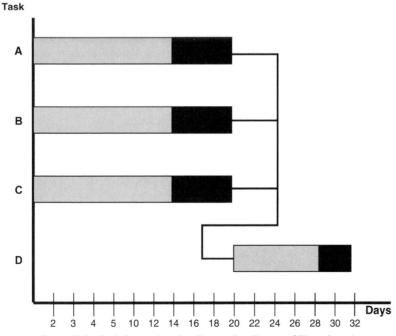

FIGURE 5.5. Task Dependencies Preventing Reuse of Time Saved

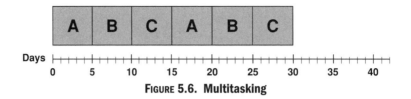

FIGURE 5.6. Multitasking

hit problems, we cannot make use of the time saved on C because it is usually impractical to reassign the free developer to the failing tasks, and D can't be started until these are complete.

So we never reap the rewards of early completion. Even if we ever get to hear about it, our plan is not flexible enough to allow the liberated time to be supplied to the tasks that need it. Lateness, however, is propagated resolutely throughout the schedule. The best outcome we can imagine is to finish on time, never early.

Multitasking

There is one final black hole through which our contingency allowances can disappear. Figure 5.6 shows a set of three tasks, each of ten days' duration. We are attempting to work on all three simultaneously, or else the prioritisation of them keeps changing. The result is that each task takes twenty days to complete— from the time we start to work on it until it is finished. If we had a consistent prioritisation and eliminated the multitasking, the lead times would shorten, as shown by Figure 5.7. Task A is now ready after ten days, not twenty, and Task B is finished five days earlier. And this is without taking into account the disruption caused by switching from one task to another.

Now let's add some contingency, say a 40 percent allowance, into the comparison, as shown by Figure 5.8. All we have done is make the problem worse. Although each task was given four days' contingency, the lead time for task A increased by *eight* days. And the more contingency we add, the worse it gets—making contingency a liability, not a safety device.

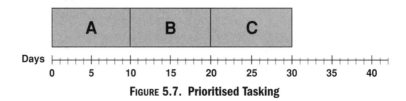

FIGURE 5.7. Prioritised Tasking

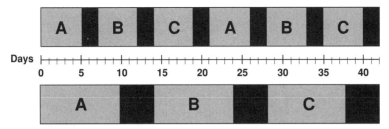

FIGURE 5.8. Adding Contingency to the Multitasking Comparison

So we need to eliminate multitasking from our schedules and make sure each team or resource has one consistent stream of prioritised work. This means that we must not plan for resources to be assigned to more than one task at a time, and we must not keep switching priorities from task to task, like a circus performer trying to spin dozens of plates simultaneously.

BUFFERING THE CONTINGENCY

Dr. Goldratt's solution to the problems of disappearing contingency is to remove the allowance from each task and to package this time as **buffers** at key points in the schedule, protecting the end-date against any delays to individual tasks. Student syndrome is removed, because the time allocated for each task is the base estimate, not the "with contingency" value. And because the contingency is aggregated, any time saved through early completion can be offset against delays to other tasks.

In an earlier chapter, I introduced Goldratt's idea of the Critical Chain, and derived this for the example shown in Figure 5.9. Multitasking has been eliminated from this plan, so removing the last of our contingency black holes.

Goldratt's method is to add a **Project Buffer** that protects the end-date against overruns on tasks in the Critical Chain. It is placed after the last task in the chain. There may also be overruns in chains that link to the Critical Chain. An additional **Feeding Buffer** is added at the end of each such chain. The buffers are shown in Figure 5.10.

Sizing the Buffers

Clearly, the placing of the contingency buffers, and the size of them, is crucial. And we also need to consider the resourcing of the buffers—is a buffer of six

Task

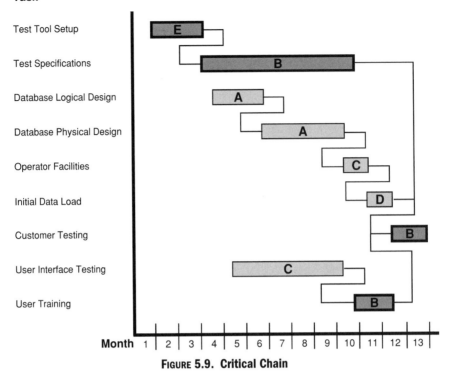

FIGURE 5.9. Critical Chain

Task

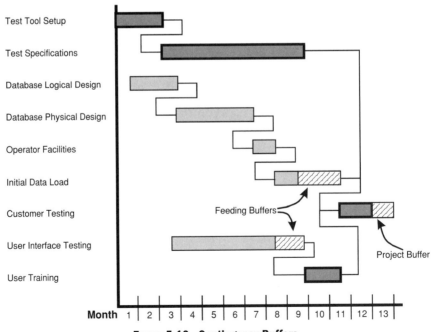

FIGURE 5.10. Contingency Buffers

88

people for one week the same as a buffer of one person for six weeks? In his book *Project Management in the Fast Lane*, Robert Newbold suggests sizing each task such that there is a 50 percent chance of its estimated duration being achieved and then asserts that each buffer should be sized at 50 percent of the length of the chain that feeds it. I have some difficulties with this approach. Firstly, it is hard to estimate something at a 50 percent confidence level—it is easier to assess how long a task will take if nothing goes wrong and then look at the assumptions you have made to derive that figure. Secondly, it is likely that some task chains are riskier than others, so a uniform contingency allowance will lead to inaccuracies. Newbold has some statistical solutions to this difficulty, but given that we already have some contingency values in our Cost Model, I prefer to use these. The method is as follows:

- Allocate all the project-wide contingency to the Project Buffer.
- For tasks that are in the Critical Chain, add their task-level contingencies to the Project Buffer as well.
- For other tasks, add the task-level contingency to the Feeding Buffer for their chain.

In the Cost Model, buffers can be entered as individual tasks, being resourced and scheduled as for any other.

Resourcing of the buffers depends on how many people are working on the relevant chain—normally they will all be assigned to the buffer. As a rule of thumb, I would say that there should not be more people than elapsed weeks assigned to a buffer. So if you determine that a buffer of sixty person-days is appropriate, it cannot have a shorter elapsed time than four weeks (for three people). If this limitation cannot be met then you may need to increase the team size or the project timeframe—the contingency allowances cannot be arbitrarily reduced.

Practical Considerations

This is a radically different way of planning and managing a project. You cannot just lop a few months off the timescale, claiming that you will be using Critical Chain techniques, and then run your projects as before. We have already experienced such over-optimism in the early days of Rapid Application Development techniques, where huge reductions in development times were anticipated from teams unfamiliar with the concepts. Only when you have planned and managed a few projects in a new way will you see if and where any savings can be made.

Planning using Critical Chain techniques will not necessarily reduce the estimated project duration. Or, to put it another way, the method will produce a more realistic schedule because the hidden penalties of student syndrome and multitasking are removed. But if any task is completed early, we will consume less from the buffers, recycling the time saved to offset any delays that arise elsewhere. Also, there are some techniques that will reduce the risk of resources becoming idle waiting for others to finish, that I describe in Chapter 8 ("Maintaining the Model"). Given all this, you could argue that the contingency can be reduced—we can assume that some tasks will complete early and that we will be able to utilise the gains made when they do. I leave that decision to you.

There are two dangers. Firstly, the development team may feel their safety factor is being eroded and start to pad their base estimates with additional contingency. They need to understand that the contingency has been redistributed, not eliminated, and that they are allowed to finish "late" so long as they apply the maximum effort. The second danger is that the contingency buffers are exposed in schedules—managers or customers may think these can be arbitrarily axed or reduced or that time can be saved through multitasking. The project manager, the development team, and all the other stakeholders must be trained to understand how Critical Chain techniques will bring increased accuracy to the estimates and better control over the project.

COMPOUNDING THE CONTINGENCY

I just mentioned the tendency of management or customers to see contingency allowances as providing potential for savings on the project cost. They affect to presume that contingency is some padding that the development team builds into their estimate in order to secure an easy time. "We will manage the risk" is a phrase I often hear, as if that somehow ensures that the hazards will be avoided and the corresponding delays won't arise. Another favourite reaction on seeing the contingency allowances is, "you are planning to fail." As we have seen, with no contingency we are left with the minimum duration the project could possibly take. Only the most suicidal would start with such an assumption. But they will still try—planning to fail, indeed.

However, you should not weight the estimates with secret contingency allowances to compensate for the real amounts that you feel may be axed. Whatever the pressures, you must insist that contingency is an inseparable element of the estimates. If the predicted risks don't happen, the project will finish early and everyone will be happy; if they do happen then we have made the best allowance we could. You can only reduce the contingency if someone can set your mind at rest about the assumptions you have made or the doubts you have. Your job is to present the most accurate figures that you are able—just make sure that any kamikaze management actions are well documented and laid at the door of those responsible.

Management over-pessimism is equally likely. You present an estimate to your manager, who adds his or her own safety margin before proffering it at the next level up. By the time the estimate is ready for signoff, it has swelled to an impossible figure. Indeed, it is quite possible for both effects to be in operation—lower level management inflate the estimates to compensate for the cuts they know will be demanded at the higher echelons. I don't have an answer to all this, but I don't recommend bending your own estimates to get the result you think is right.

CHAPTER 6

Costing the Project

In spite of the cost of living, it's still popular.
—*Laurence J. Peter*

STAFF COSTS

Project Roles

To cost the project we need to determine each project role, the amount of time for which that role is needed, and the daily cost of a person with the skills to fill it.

Some possible roles to consider are the following:

- project manager
- "keeper of the vision"
- functional authority
- technical manager
- quality inspectors
- database design experts
- test database manager
- system manager
- team leaders
- experienced analyst/programmers

- junior analyst/programmers
- consultants with specific knowledge
- packaged software specialists
- performance analysts
- prototype developers
- user interface designers
- test team leader
- test team members
- technical writers

For each role, you must determine the following:

- how many such people are needed
- when they will be needed
- for how long they will be needed
- who they are going to report to, in terms of line management and for technical guidance
- whether they can be used at any earlier or later points (e.g., can technical specification writer number 2 become team leader number 4 later in the project?)
- the name of the person who will fill the role, if you know it

Ideal and Actual Staff

All project roles require different mixtures of skills and experience. It is important that we assign the right grade of staff to each task so we cost the project accurately. We can take two approaches:

1. Treat the estimate as an academic exercise and price a hypothetical, ideally qualified person to each logical role. As the project develops, assume that new, ideally-qualified staff will appear, taking up the roles needed later in the life cycle.
2. Assume continuity of staff between the different phases of the project, presupposing that they have a mixture of skills and can move from role to role.

In most cases, the second approach is more pragmatic, especially if the known pool of staff is limited or a team has already been earmarked for the project.

However, this can lead to situations where there is "slack time" for some team members, because they cannot start in a new role until some other work is complete. This should be included in the plan and may provide part of a contingency buffer if you are using this method.

If you don't have the actual names of the proposed project staff, you could name a real person who you know would be ideal for each role. It doesn't matter if he or she is working in Bangalore and unlikely to be free until doomsday. Just say to yourself "we need a 'Jane Smith' sort of person here and a 'Bill Jones' sort of person there." As actual individuals replace these ideals, keep an eye on their experience and skills. A cheaper team may cut down the cost, but maybe the contingency should be increased. Conversely, it is wrong to assume that higher-grade staff will do a faster job. They may do a better one (so you may care to reduce the contingency), but task duration is not proportional to seniority.

If you are assuming that a person with a particular mix of skills will be deployed, you must consider a contingency allowance for the risk that nobody suitable will appear, or that the specific person you had in mind will not be available, and you have to make do with someone less flexible.

Finally, remember the Critical Chain. We do not want the same person to be working on two tasks at once, for we have seen the effects of multitasking on completion times. But if we eliminate such resource dependencies, the Critical Chain will lengthen and our planned end-date will start to move out. It is important to be prepared to change your "ideal" plan, for it will mutate as real people are nominated to fill each role.

The Staff Plan

Consideration of the project roles should enable you to complete the Staff Plan in the Cost Model, showing the assignment of each individual to each task. The result for the example project is shown in Figure 6.1.

		Total Days			Aug-02	Sep-02	Oct-02	Nov-02	Dec-02	Jan-03	Feb-03	Mar-03	Apr-03
			Staff Profile		4	4	4	4.5	5	4.5	3.5	1	0.5
		591	Total Days		76	76	76	86	95	86	67	19	10
	Check From Tasks sheet	593	Check		76	76	77	86	95	86	67	19	10
Role	**Name**	**Days**											
Project Manager	Antony Lamont	133			19	19	19	19	19	19	19		
Analyst/Programmer 1	Dee Selby or similar	133			19	19	19	19	19	19	19		
Analyst/Programmer 2	Ditto	114			19	19	19	19	19	19			
Analyst/Programmer 3	Phillip Mathers or similar	115			19	19	19	19	19	10	10		
Integrator/Tester	John Divney or similar	96						10	19	19	19	19	10

FIGURE 6.1. Staff Plan

Once you have decided on the project roles, the Staff Plan is not too difficult to derive from the Tasks sheet. A check row shows that totals in the two sheets tally for each month.

Here I have assumed that the same people write the specifications and the code, while another person undertakes the integration and testing. Only the Project Manager has been nominated so far; for the remaining roles I have named people who have the appropriate experience and skills so that I can determine a cost.

Daily Rates

Now we need a daily cost for each of the staff members or roles that we have decided to allocate to our project. For software house and contractor staff, this is easy because their rates are known. Internal staff are more of a problem because most organisations have not calculated how much each employee really costs them per day. Factors to be included in the daily rate include the following:

- the employee's salary
- their pension, allowances, expenses, fringe benefits, and so on
- the employer's contribution to taxes (e.g., National Insurance in the United Kingdom)
- office costs (e.g., rent, heating, lighting, cleaning, insurance, communications, equipment, and software)
- support staff (e.g., secretaries, human resources, and accounts)—all their salaries, benefits, office costs, and so on
- line management—not only their salaries and costs but also those of the support staff they use

You may be able to get a total of your organisation's operating costs from your accounts department and divide this by the number of "chargeable" staff—by which I mean those who may be directly deployed on a project. However, this method does not distinguish between the different roles and may introduce inaccuracies if a project calls for a mix of staff that is particularly skilled or particularly unskilled. A more precise measure is obtained by assigning the total operating costs *pro rata* according to the salary of each employee. This yields a specific daily rate for each of the "chargeable" staff. You can then derive a typical rate for each role, such as a project manager or a C++ programmer, which can be used to cost projects whose specific team members are not yet known.

		Total Days	Average Rate	Cost (USD)
		591	676	400860
	Check From Tasks sheet	593		

Role	Name	Days	Rate	USD
Project Manager	Antony Lamont	133	890	118370
Analyst/Programmer 1	Dee Selby or similar	133	670	89110
Analyst/Programmer 2	Ditto	114	670	76380
Analyst/Programmer 3	Phillip Mathers or similar	115	600	69000
Integrator/Tester	John Divney or similar	96	500	48000

FIGURE 6.2. Staff Cost Sheet

It is particularly important to use accurate daily rates when comparing the "in-house" cost of a project with a price quoted by an external organisation. I have seen cases where the internal project cost was simply defined as the sum of the team's salaries for the estimated duration, and this then compared with a software house price that included all of their operational costs as well as a contingency allowance and mark-up. This proves nothing. If you want to see the true cost/benefit picture then you must have accurate rates for staff time—both to determine the development costs and to evaluate the gains that the project will bring in terms of improved efficiency, redeployment, deskilling, or whatever.

Once we insert the rates into the Cost Model, we can derive a total staff cost, as shown in Figure 6.2.

This sheet also shows the *average* daily rate—the total staff cost divided by the total number of days. This figure is sometimes useful to make quick assessments when you are asked awkward questions like, "how much would we save if we didn't print any reports?"

CAPITAL COSTS

Types of Capital Cost Items

By "capital costs" I mean expenditure on items other than the project staff—things like the following:

- processors and peripherals
- communications equipment
- software licences
- hardware and system software support
- line rentals

- installation and support
- the hardware environment (e.g., machine rooms and air conditioning)
- insurance
- consumables
- printing and binding
- travel and accommodation
- training courses
- beers

These are sometimes called "fixed costs" or "capital expenses." I know that, strictly speaking, some of these items are not capital costs, but it is the best term I can think of.

For the major items, you may have obtained quotations from suppliers; for others you will need to make an estimate. It could be that some costs are directly proportional to the duration of some phase of the project—for example, if the team needs to be accommodated in a hotel or is being paid a daily site allowance. Such dependencies can be reflected in the Cost Model.

Reclaimable taxes, such as VAT in Europe, are not usually included in quoted prices. So remove this from quotations from suppliers and contractors, telling your customer that the price excludes such tax. Taxes that cannot be reclaimed, such as customs duties, should be included in the costs.

Contingency must be considered for the capital costs. For example, if you have a hardware quotation from a reputable supplier, you may consider this as risk free; but suppose you find you have forgotten a few items or the supplier suddenly quotes a later delivery date? In the same way that we distinguished between task contingency and project contingency earlier, we will apply a contingency allowance to individual items on the capital costs list, as well as a project-wide contingency. The latter is determined by those elements of the Risk Analysis that needed to be estimated in money terms, and will be averaged out over the all the capital cost items, as we did for the tasks.

Basic Details

In the Cost Model we can prepare the Capital Costs worksheet. There are many columns to this sheet, so I deal with them in sections. Firstly, there are the basic details about the item, as shown in Table 6.1.

For the example project, these elements are shown in Figure 6.3.

TABLE 6.1. Capital Costs Basic Details	
Reference	A reference number. This normally just starts at 1, but could be used to record manufacturers' part numbers or suppliers' quotation numbers.
Item	A brief description of the capital cost item. If the item is defined elsewhere (e.g., a supplier's quotation) then just reference that.
Supplier	The name of the supplier of the item, if known.
Notes	Any further details, such as how the cost or item contingency has been determined.

Costs and Contingency

Now we can turn to the cost and contingency columns, described in Table 6.2. For the example project, these elements are shown in Figure 6.4.

You may wish to carry forward some values from other places in the Cost Model to fill the "Quantity" column. In the example, I calculated the total number of days to be spent installing and testing the system at the customer's offices on the "Scratchpad" sheet and set this as the "Quantity" for Item 2. The daily payment made to the team for working away from home (the "On-site allowance") is also entered and named on the Scratchpad—such constants should always be explicit rather than hidden in the workbook calculations. The number of days to be spent on site already has a contingency allowance built in, and there is no additional risk because the allowance rate is preset.

I have a fixed and irrevocable quotation for the hardware, and the amount allowed for Item 4 should be more than enough, so I'm not going to make any contingency allowance for these. However, for the software licence in Item 3, I have a worry because I can only obtain last year's price, so I have made a contingency allowance in case this has increased.

Ref	Item	Supplier	Notes
1	Development and target hardware	Babbage Ltd.	Quotation DFR37353282
2	On-site allowances		For on-site testing period
3	Licence for EntityViewer design tool	Entity Corp.	Last year's price
4	Consumables		

FIGURE 6.3. Example Capital Costs Basic Details

TABLE 6.2. Capital Costs and Contingency	
Cost	The unit cost of the item.
Quantity	The number of the items that will be needed.
Base Cost	"Cost" × "Quantity."
Item Contingency	The contingency allowance for this item.
Project Contingency	The cost inclusive of the project-wide contingency, expressed in money terms, from the Risk Analysis.

We now need to factor in the project-wide contingency for the risks that were evaluated in terms of cost. The procedure is the same as for risks assessed in terms of days, where an amount is added to each task. In the example, the Risk Analysis shows $3,929 is to be added, so I manipulated the project-wide contingency percentage until I got as close as I could to this. Thus 11.95 percent is added to all the capital costs to give a project contingency of $3,926, which is near enough.

Depreciated and Built-In Costs

So far, there has been little difference in the costing method to be adopted for developments internal to an organisation, and those undertaken by an external business, like a software house. However, when it comes to the capital costs there are two possible approaches:

	Base Total	25706			
	Item Contingency		27.8%	7150	USD
	Total with Item Contingency			32856	
	Project Contingency		11.95%	3929	3926
	Total Capital Costs (USD)			36782	

Ref	Item	Cost (USD)	Qty.	Base Cost	Item Cont. %	Item Cont. USD	Total (USD)
1	Development and target hardware	23456	1	23456		23456	26259
2	On-site allowances	250	29	7250		7250	8116
3	Licence for EntityViewer design tool	1000	1	1000	15%	1150	1287
4	Consumables	1000	1	1000		1000	1120

FIGURE 6.4. Example Capital Costs and Contingency

1. We can depreciate the cost of each item over a number of years, which usually has advantages for tax purposes. The simplest method is "straight-line depreciation" whereby the eventual salvage value of the item is subtracted from the original cost and the result then distributed equally over the expected service life. Your organisation will probably have a policy about how the depreciation should be handled for various types of equipment, and these should be considered alongside any rules imposed by the tax authorities.

2. We can build the capital costs into those of the initial software development project. This approach is more suitable for a software house attempting to determine the price of a "turnkey" solution. Such organisations are not too concerned with how their customers manage their accounting or tax affairs, but will be interested in the schedule of expenses incurred relative to income received.

According to which method you wish to adopt for each capital cost item, within the Cost Model you should complete one of the sets of columns described in Table 6.3.

TABLE 6.3. Depreciation or Inclusion of Capital Costs		
Method	Cost Model Columns	Contents
Costs to be Depreciated	Depreciation Start Date	The month at which depreciation should start—usually when the item is delivered.
	Depreciation Years	The number of years over which the item should be depreciated—usually one, three, or five.
Costs to be Included Within the Initial Project	Monthly Allocations	The month or months within the project timescale in which the item's cost will be incurred. This may be when the item is delivered, when the bill for it will be received, or when the bill will be paid.

		Total (USD) 36782	Initial Costs 10523	Depreciated Costs 26283										

						Included in Project Costs								
Ref	Item	Total (USD)	Check	Depreciate From	Years	Aug-02 1447	Sep-02 160	Oct-02 160	Nov-02 160	Dec-02 160	Jan-03 160	Feb-03 160	Mar-03 5317	Apr-03 2799
1	Development and target hardware	26259	26283	Aug-02	3									
2	On-site allowances	8116	8116										5317	2799
3	Licence for EntityViewer design tool	1287	1287			1287								
4	Consumables	1120	1120			160	160	160	160	160	160	160		

FIGURE 6.5. Example Capital Costs Allocation

For the example project, I have decided to depreciate the hardware over three years, but I will factor the remaining capital costs into the initial development, as shown in Figure 6.5. Item 1 has been depreciated, and later we see how this appears in the ongoing costs for the project. The "check" column differs slightly from the cost itself, owing to rounding errors.

For the costs to be included within the initial project, Item 3 is needed right at the start, so I will take the full hit then. If I knew that we always delay paying the bills for such items, I could postpone the allocation. The on-site allowance is only going to be paid in March and April, so I allocated the cost proportionally to the number of days to be worked in these months. Finally, I distributed the cost of consumables evenly over the design and development phases.

ONGOING COSTS

The cost of a new system continues to grow after it is accepted or put into operational use. If you are estimating the cost of a "turnkey" solution on behalf of a software house, you may not be too concerned with any expenses your customer may incur after your bills are paid, but any sensible cost/benefit analysis of an internal project will include a cost projection over the first few years of operational life, at the least. Typical ongoing costs include the following:

- capital cost items you have decided to depreciate
- hardware maintenance
- system software maintenance (e.g., yearly licence fees or the cost of upgrading to new versions as they are released)
- bespoke software maintenance (e.g., bug fixes and upgrades)
- operations (e.g., data centres and staff)

	Total	2002	2003	2004	2005	2006	2007
Depreciation of Capital Costs	26283	3667	8747	8771	5098		
Other Ongoing Costs	201250		40250	40250	40250	40250	40250
Total Ongoing Costs	227533	3667	48997	49021	45348	40250	40250

Ref	Item	Rate USD	Total Days	Total USD	Days					
	STAFF COSTS				2002	2003	2004	2005	2006	2007
1	Operations (0.5 days/week)	650	125	81250		25	25	25	25	25
2	Data Preparation (1 day/week)	450	250	112500		50	50	50	50	50
	Total (Days)		375			75	75	75	75	75
	Total (USD)			193750		38750	38750	38750	38750	38750

Ref	Item	Total (USD)	USD					
	OTHER COSTS		2002	2003	2004	2005	2006	2007
3	Hardware maintenance (quotation from Babbage Ltd)	6000		1500	1500	1500	1500	1500
	Total	6000		1500	1500	1500	1500	1500

FIGURE 6.6. Ongoing Costs

- data preparation
- post-acceptance support

In the Cost Model, these are reflected in the Ongoing Costs sheet. For the example project, I have extrapolated costs for the next five years, as shown in Figure 6.6.

For staff costs, enter the rates and the number of days that will be needed for each role per year. In the year in which the project is completed, this will often be a reduced amount, or zero. Also, the effort needed may tail off gradually as the application becomes established.

Where the ongoing costs cannot be evaluated in terms of person-days, the other section of the worksheet should be used, entering the cost of each item per year.

COST SUMMARY

The Summary sheet brings together the Staff Costs, the Capital Costs, and the Ongoing Costs. For the example project, it is shown in Figure 6.7.

COST SUMMARY
Example Project

	Total (USD)	2002	2003	2004	2005	2006	2007
Staff Costs	400860	283350	117510				
Capital Costs	10523	2087	8436				
Total Initial Cost	411383	285437	125946				
Ongoing Costs	227533	3667	48997	49021	45348	40250	40250
Total Project Cost	638916	289104	174943	49021	45348	40250	40250

FIGURE 6.7. Summary Sheet

At long last, we have the total initial cost of the project, and a grand total that includes the ongoing costs, if this is needed. I guarantee that these totals will be a great deal higher than you, or anyone else, thought they were going to be. I also guarantee that unless you have made an error in the calculations somewhere, this is the amount the project *will* cost. At least. So if you, your management, or your customers start to chip away at these totals, you are only fooling yourselves. If you get some new information—maybe to set your mind at rest about a few of the risks—then the model can be adjusted. But not just because the cost seems so unexpectedly high.

CASHFLOW

For internal company projects your estimate is now done. You have the project cost, and now you or your superiors must decide if the benefits will outweigh those costs. However, if you work for a software house, and are charging for the cost of the project, there is one more stage—to determine your profit margin and when to bill.

Your own company procedures will determine the assessment of an appropriate margin. The Cashflow sheet, shown in Figure 6.8, determines the cumulative costs and the cumulative amount billed and so reveals the amount by which the project is in profit or loss on a month-by-month basis. For the example, I am going to add a modest 25 percent mark-up to the project cost.

Here I am defining the billing profile as 50 percent at the start of the project, 25 percent at the start of December, and the final 25 percent as the system enters its final support phase in March. I am assuming (somewhat optimistically) that it takes a month for our bills to be paid, so I will credit these amounts to the month following submission. The sheet shows the amount of each bill, the price (total income), the profit margin (profit as a percentage of price), and the monthly cashflow.

The ideal is to keep the cashflow in the black all the way along, but as this means billing well in advance of anything being delivered or visible to

	Total (USD)	Check	Aug-02	Sep-02	Oct-02	Nov-02	Dec-02	Jan-03	Feb-03	Mar-03	Apr-03
Staff Costs (USD)	400860		53770	53770	53770	58770	63270	57870	45140	9500	5000
Capital Costs (USD)	10523		1447	160	160	160	160	160	160	5317	2799
Total Costs (USD)	411383		55217	53930	53930	58930	63430	58030	45300	14817	7799
Billing Schedule		100.00%		50.00%				25.00%			25.00%
Markup	25.00%										
Income (USD)	514229	514229		257114				128557			128557
Gross Profit (USD)	102846	Cashflow	-55217	147967	94037	35107	-28323	42205	-3095	-17912	102846
Margin	20.00%										

FIGURE 6.8. Cashflow Sheet

the customer, this is usually difficult to negotiate A **neutral cashflow** means that the bottom line is always zero—again often hard to negotiate, although theoretically fair. Usually, the situation is as shown in the example, with the cashflow bouncing between credit and debit.

PRICE BREAKDOWN

It is common for managers or customers to ask for a price breakdown, showing individual cost elements. An attribution of the costs allows them to decide which parts of the overall system they may wish to implement, delay, or cancel. Indeed, support for such decisions is often why we undertook the estimate in the first place. However, producing a breakdown is a problem, because the proportion of the overall cost is not easy to attribute to individual tasks, owing to factors such as overheads and the project-wide contingency. We must make sure that if individual items are "cherry-picked" then their true cost is accurately represented. Also, in a commercial environment, we won't want customers to see our profit margin, so we must factor this back into the attribution of the overall cost to each task.

Fortunately, we have an estimate of the number of days for each task that includes the project-wide contingency. We need to bolster these values *pro rata* with the effort for the overhead tasks. For the example project, the Price Breakdown is shown in Figure 6.9.

Under "Cost to be Attributed", enter the amount you wish to divide between the various tasks. In this case, I have entered the total price to the customer. In the "Cost Element" column, indicate with a "Y" those tasks amongst which you wish this amount to be distributed. The effort needed for all other tasks is

		Cost Elements	221			
		Other Tasks	372			**USD**
		Total	**593**	Cost Actually Attributed		514228
		Check from Tasks sheet	593	Cost to be Attributed		**514229**
		Cost			Weighted	
Ref	Task	Element?	Days		Days	Cost
A	Code and Unit Test					
A1	Input Screens	Y	77		207	179503
A2	Database Schemas	Y	30		80	69373
A3	Reports	Y	45		121	104927
A4	Usage Stats	Y	69		185	160425
B	Overheads					
B1	Project Management		133			
B2	Specifications		133			
B3	Integration and Testing		106			

FIGURE 6.9. Price Breakdown

then used to weight the number of days estimated for the tasks selected, and the cost is allocated in proportion to this. A breakdown of the cost of each selected element then appears in the right-hand column.

This approach assumes that the capital costs are attributable *pro rata* among the tasks selected. It also assumes that team skills are contributed in proportion to the size of each task, which would be misleading for tasks that need staff who are particularly skilled, or particularly unskilled. So the Price Breakdown can only be considered as a rough guide to the cost of each selected task. If your management or customers decided to do without the "Usage Stats", for example, you would really need to evaluate the whole estimate again, rather than knock $160,425 off the price.

VISUALISING THE MODEL

Using Microsoft Excel to construct the Cost Model makes it easy to produce some diagrams. With the data from the example, I can show the staffing profile (Figure 6.10), the price breakdown (Figure 6.11), and the monthly costs, billing, and cashflow (Figure 6.12).

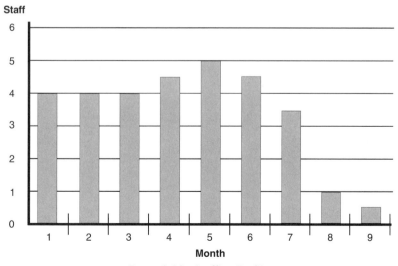

FIGURE **6.10. Staffing Profile**

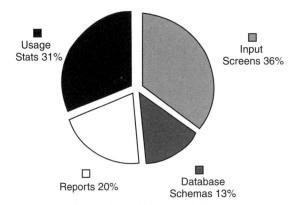

FIGURE 6.11. Price Breakdown

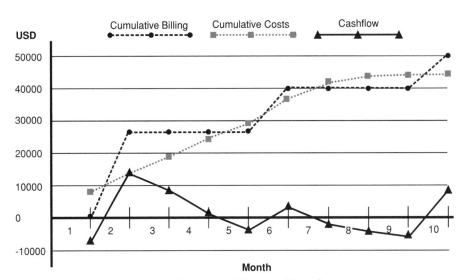

FIGURE 6.12. Costs, Billing, and Cashflow

CHAPTER 7

Reviewing the Estimates

In judging others, folks will work overtime for no pay.
—*Charles Edwin Carruthers*

TIDYING UP

Before submitting your estimate for review, you should run through all the sheets in the Cost Model one last time to make sure they are complete, consistent, and correct. Check that the sheets are tidy and that you feel you can justify all the figures. Are you satisfied with the contingency allowances? Are the estimates and contingency consistent between the different tasks? Are there any glaring errors in the calculation of totals? Dare you let someone else see the finished result?

Now, some sort of review of your estimate is essential, not to spread the blame and reduce your estimidity, but just to get someone to point out the factors you have overlooked. So we come to Rule 11.

> **Blindingly Obvious Rule of Estimation Number 11**
> *Have someone else review your estimate.*

If a review cannot be undertaken for some reason, you have a new risk and a potential addition to the project contingency.

TYPES OF REVIEW

There are several possible approaches to the review process; the advantages and disadvantages of each are described below.

Parallel Estimate by a Peer

This is the ideal method, having the advantage of showing up tasks, concerns, or assumptions that were forgotten by the other person. If the estimates are both conducted using the "bottom-up" method I describe in this book, the estimators can first agree the lists of tasks and risks. The estimates themselves can then be conducted separately, before the base figures and contingency allowances are compared. Planning and costing can then be a combined effort using the task durations agreed between the two estimators.

If two different estimation methods are employed, a problem arises in presenting the figures in a form that can be validly compared. It might seem that more accuracy would be achieved if the problem is tackled from several different directions, but this is only true if the underlying reasons for any disparities can be exposed.

Either way, the crunch point comes if there are widely differing views on the effort required for one or more tasks. The estimid way out is to take the higher one each time. Worse still, a manager or customer may decide to be optimistic and take the *lower* figure from each pair. All this must be fought. If the method of parallel estimation is to be of use, the comparison must be thought out on a task-by-task basis, possibly monitored by a third party. It is usually the case that one of the estimators has a greater depth of knowledge of the application than the other and should take the final responsibility to combine the figures.

Peer Review of an Existing Estimate

Here the estimate is completed by one person and then reviewed by another of equal or greater experience. The snag is that the reviewer usually does not have the in-depth application knowledge of the estimator and gets a panic attack of estimidity. All the figures are bumped up a bit, so everyone feels comfortable, but the project never starts. Worse still, the estimator may refuse to alter his or her original figures, leaving the reviewer as a Cassandra, muttering, "I think it's all hopelessly underestimated but no one will listen."

To avoid these situations, a peer review should be treated as a chance for the reviewer to raise queries and points that the original estimator may need to consider. The estimator can take these factors on board if they wish, without the ability to shift the responsibility on to the reviewer. Even if the reviewer still has serious doubts about the figures, the person with the in-depth knowledge should take the final responsibility for them.

Team Estimate from a List of Tasks

Having agreed the list of tasks, a team—usually senior members of the proposed development project—tries to agree an estimate for each. In my experience, there are two scenarios:

1. One person in the team dominates the effort and takes the key decisions, such as the estimation of a baseline task. The rest of the team then breathe a sigh of relief and complete the easy bits. In times of trouble, it is all the fault of the pathfinder, while everyone else claims to have raised doubts that were not heeded. The benefits of teamwork are thus negated.
2. Everyone is too estimid to venture any opinions. Anyone who is foolish enough to name a figure is immediately overruled by others who want it increased. The eventual estimate spirals, ending up so overcautious that it is useless.

So this method is not effective unless there is strong leader who can achieve agreement while still drawing on the combined skills and experience of the team.

Wideband-Delphi

This Delphi technique was developed by the RAND Corporation in the 1940s and extended by Barry Boehm. It resembles the team estimate described above but avoids the problems. The estimation team first meet to agree the project goals and assumptions. They then each make an individual list of project tasks and undertake the size estimates. These lists are given to a moderator, who tabulates the results and returns them to the team. Only the member's own estimate is identified—all others are anonymous. The team then meet again to discuss the result, after which each member may choose to revise his or her own estimate. The cycle continues until the numbers converge to within an acceptable range.

The advantages are that the team knowledge is pooled, without the risk of one member intimidating the rest into seeing things their way. It might obtain agreement between widely differing opinions. The disadvantages lie in holding a discussion that remains anonymous—if your figure is different from the rest, how can you argue for it without identifying yourself?

I hold such reviews in at least two stages. The first is to reach a consensus on the list of tasks; the next is to agree the estimates and contingency for each item on the list. Further stages may cover the risks and commercial terms in cases where these are significant issues.

Combined Walk-through and Estimate

This combines a technical review with a team estimate. Each task is described by someone (maybe the system architect), and then two or more people write down their figures for the estimate. These are then revealed, compared, discussed, and agreed. Such a process allows concerns, both technical and organisational, to be raised and fully discussed in context, revealing assumptions and risks.

The method can suffer the disadvantages of the team review, mentioned earlier, but is inherently more collaborative, concentrating on technical issues that the team can freely discuss, before tackling the more contentious aspects of the estimate itself. In my experience, the process works very well. The only snag is that the exercise can take several tiring days—although this is offset by the amount of understanding that is achieved by the technical walk-through.

SIGNOFF

Once the estimate has been reviewed and revised, the next stage is usually a higher-level presentation to your management or customers. You must be prepared to answer questions concerning how the price or timescale can be reduced, the cost of each subcomponent, the effect of removing various tasks, the justification of the contingency, and your general faith in the accuracy of the estimate. Rarely, in my experience, are the base estimates affected by such reviews, but some assumptions may be questioned and the contingency altered. All being well, the estimate will be approved and your job is done; more often, there is at least one revision before everyone is happy.

The Cost Model's header sheet has spaces for a formal signoff by each stake-holder, if that is your procedure.

CHAPTER 8

Maintaining the Model

Plans get you into things, but you got to work your way out.
—*Will Rogers*

WHY BOTHER?

This is not a book about project management, but I want to show how the figures we have derived in order to cost a system can continue to be of value as development proceeds.

Let's be honest. At the start of a project, our understanding of it is fuzzy at best. As the work progresses, the assignment, and its associated problems, comes into greater focus. Only at the end do we fully understand what we were doing. And the estimates will reflect this. Before we start, we will get widely differing opinions on the effort needed. Only on the day we complete the system, when the champagne is flowing and the customers are wheeling in barrow-loads of money to reward our efforts (I like to dream sometimes), do we know exactly how much it all cost.

Our estimate starts wrong (Rule 1) and ends up 100 percent right, so it must continually improve as the implementation proceeds. But only if we keep the Cost Model up to date. Too often, the original estimate is ignored once the work starts, or is just given the occasional passing kick. In fact, it is the most valuable tool the Project Manager possesses, for if the model is well maintained,

FIGURE 8.1. Today's Crossword

trends can be spotted, risks headed off, change well managed, and costs controlled.

PROBLEMS WITH PROGRESS REPORTING

After thirty minutes of brow-furrowing work today, Figure 8.1 shows my attempt at today's crossword. How far have I got, and how long will it take me to do the rest? I seem to have completed around three-quarters of it, so another ten minutes and I should be done. But hold on. Those unfinished answers have the toughest clues—I have already attempted them, and failed. In fact, right now I couldn't tell you when, or even if, I will be able to finish this puzzle.

Project progress reporting suffers the same problem. It concentrates on completed tasks, documenting success month after month until only a few tasks are left—the tough, late ones. Suddenly, progress seems to have slowed, or stopped, even though these tasks have been there, causing problems, all along. Your reports will demonstrate the truth observed by Frederick P. Brooks in *The Mythical Man-Month*—the first 90 percent of the work takes 90 percent of the time, and the remaining 10 percent takes the *other* 90 percent.

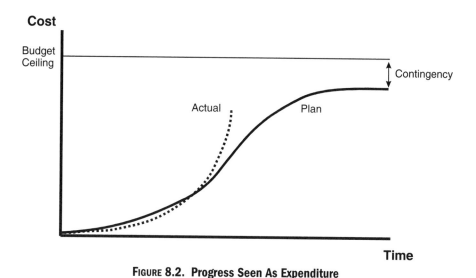

FIGURE 8.2. Progress Seen As Expenditure

On the other hand, you cannot monitor progress just by looking at costs. Figure 8.2 shows a chart plotting actual expenditure against that planned in order to obtain a view of the current project status. The chart shows that we are going over budget, but we cannot see why. Maybe we are making great progress but with a high "burn rate", or maybe we are deploying extra resources to maintain a failing schedule. And we cannot see the individual components that are causing the deviation.

So we need some way to analyse both the work expended and the progress made so far, comparing this with the planned effort shown in the Cost Model. Then we can report status clearly and accurately, recalibrating the model as we go along. One method to achieve this is termed **Earned Value Management**, the principles of which I describe below. It could be that you have your own local standards for project status reporting, but if these allow failing tasks to be hidden by the success of others, or they concentrate on effort expended rather than results achieved, I suggest you campaign to get them revised.

EARNED VALUE MANAGEMENT

Principles

Earned Value Management is a technique for determining the cost and schedule performance of a project. It is a part of the U.S. Department of Defense

Cost/Schedule Control System Criteria to standardise contractor requirements for reporting progress.

The principle is that tasks "earn value" as they are completed. I am not talking about value in terms of business benefit here, but as a measurement of how much of the task is actually complete. By comparing this Earned Value with the planned value for a specific time period we get an indication of progress. We also evaluate the cost that has been expended to produce the Earned Value, comparing it with that planned. This gives a measure of productivity. If we have good productivity but slow progress then the task is understaffed; if productivity is low then there is probably some unplanned work to do. It's that simple—indeed you may be wondering why something so obvious merits being classed as a named technique. But if we undertake such an analysis at regular intervals, poorly performing tasks will not be hidden, we can distinguish between cost and schedule overruns, and we will see where our Cost Model needs adjustment.

Terms

To utilise Earned Value Management we must break the project down into **Work Packages**, each of which must conform to the following criteria:

1. Represent a unit of work at the level at which work is performed.
2. Be clearly distinguished from other Work Packages.
3. Be assignable to a single individual or group.
4. Have scheduled start and completion dates and interim milestones, all of which are representative of physical accomplishment.
5. Have a budget, expressed in person-days. It could also be expressed in money terms, but this would mean assigning a cost to each individual task, which is not always easy.
6. Be limited to a relatively short span of time, or be divided by discrete milestones to enable measurement of the work completed.
7. Be integrated within an overall detailed schedule that covers the entire project.

So each of the entries in our Task List is a Work Package. Overhead tasks may fail Rule 4, but I find no harm in including them, setting a milestone at the end of each reporting period. For larger projects, you could find it difficult to track *every* task, so you may prefer to group them into larger Work Packages.

Seven quantities are associated with each Work Package within a given time period as follows:

1. Budgeted Cost of Work Scheduled (*BCWS*). The planned budget for the Work Package.
2. Budgeted Cost of Work Performed (*BCWP*). The planned budget for the proportion of the Work Package actually completed.
3. Actual Cost of Work Performed (*ACWP*). The cost (in days) incurred in achieving the proportion of the Work Package actually completed.
4. Schedule Variance (*SV*). The difference between *BCWS* and *BCWP*.
5. Schedule Performance Index (*SPI*). The ratio of work completed to that planned (*BCWP* ÷ *BCWS*). An *SPI* of less than 1.0 indicates that the task is behind schedule.
6. Cost Variance (*CV*). The difference between *BCWP* and *ACWP*.
7. Cost Performance Index (*CPI*). The ratio of actual cost to planned cost (*BCWP* ÷ *ACWP*). A *CPI* of less than 1.0 indicates a cost overrun.

For example, in a particular month we planned to expend forty days on a certain Work Package. In fact, the team booked sixty days to work on that Package, but only completed 75 percent of the progress planned. So the *BCWS* is forty days, the *BCWP* is thirty days and the *ACWP* is sixty days. This yields an *SV* of ten days, a *SPI* of 0.75, a *CV* of thirty days and a *CPI* of 0.5. The situation is pictured in Figure 8.3.

By adding, we can determine the seven Earned Value metrics for any sub-component, phase, or the project as a whole. At these higher levels, we have some additional measures:

- Budget at Completion (*BAC*). The sum of all the budgets, including any contingency.
- Estimate at Completion (*EAC*). The actual costs incurred to date, plus an estimate of the cost of work remaining. There are several formulae that can be used to calculate *EAC*, which are discussed in Chapter 11 ("The Cost Model Template").

Measuring Earned Value

One of the criteria for a Work Package is the ability to measure progress as a series of milestones. This is not always easy. For example, when producing a

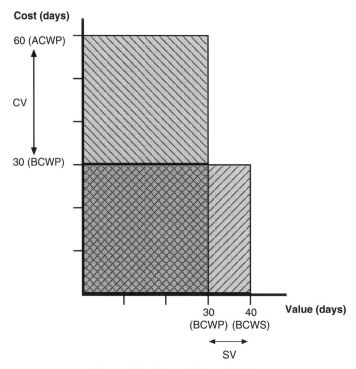

FIGURE 8.3. Earned Value Metrics

Functional Specification, we cannot say that it is 50 percent finished because six of twelve possible sections have been produced—it could be in the same situation as my attempt at today's crossword. *Earned Value Project Management* by Quentin Fleming and Joel Koppelman lists the following methods by which to measure Earned Value.

- **Weighted Milestones.** Each milestone is assigned a percentage of the budget for that Work Package, which is earned when that milestone is achieved.

- **Fixed Formula.** For example, 25 percent of the budget is earned when the Work Package is started, and the remaining 75 percent when it completes.

- **Percent-Complete Estimates.** A periodic estimate is made by the person implementing the Work Package. To prevent over-optimistic estimates, the Project Manager may assign a ceiling, say of 80 percent of the budget, and the implementer may only estimate progress within this limit. Only once the Project Manager agrees that the Work Package is complete can the remaining 20 percent be earned.

- **Percent-Complete Estimates with Milestones.** Estimates of Earned Value are allowed only up to a preset value for each milestone. For example, the first milestone may have an assignment of 30 percent of the budget, and no more than this 30 percent can be earned until some predefined criteria that define the completion of the milestone have been met.

- **Equivalent Completed Units.** A preset value is earned on completion of the Work Package.

- **Earned Standards.** Value is earned against a scale based on historical data—for example, if we know that we normally produce thirty widgets per month, we can compare current production against this baseline.

- **Apportioned Relationships to Other Work Packages**. A Work Package is valued as a proportion of another, which is used as a baseline. Progress on the baseline is also taken as a measurement of progress on the related tasks.

- **Level of Effort.** Earned Value is identical to the amount of effort expended within a given time period. This method is undesirable, but is sometimes needed for tasks that have no obvious milestones, such as project management.

You must also be able to assess the "cost" at each time period. Ideally, this is achieved through each team member submitting a timesheet listing how much effort he or she has devoted to each Work Package. If you can't employ such a process, you may have to estimate a cost.

Tracking Within the Cost Model

The Cost Model contains a sheet for tracking Earned Value. For the example project, Figure 8.4 shows how it may look at the end of month four.

Ref	Name	Aug-02 BCWS	BCWP	ACWP	Sep-02 BCWS	BCWP	ACWP	Oct-02 BCWS	BCWP	ACWP	Nov-02 BCWS	BCWP	ACWP
		76	59	79	76	76	79	77	108	103	86	117	97
A	Code and Unit Test												
A1	Input Screens										19	19	19
A2	Database Schemas							29	19	19		10	10
A3	Reports										19	45	19
A4	Usage Stats1							0	10	5	19	19	25
B	Overheads												
B1	Project Management	19	19	19	19	19	19	19	19	19	19	19	19
B2	Specifications	57	40	60	57	57	60	19	60	60			
B3	Integration and Testing										10	5	5

FIGURE 8.4. Progress on the Example Project

Ref	Name	BAC	EAC	BCWS	BCWP	ACWP	SV	SPI	CV	CPI
		593	590	315	360	358	45	1.14	2	1.01
A	Code and Unit Test									
A1	Input Screens	77	77	19	19	19	0	1.00	0	1.00
A2	Database Schemas	30	30	29	29	29	0	1.00	0	1.00
A3	Reports	45	19	19	45	19	26	2.37	26	2.37
A4	Usage Stats	69	70	29	29	30	0	1.00	-1	0.97
B	Overheads									
B1	Project Management	133	133	76	76	76	0	1.00	0	1.00
B2	Specifications	133	160	133	157	180	24	1.18	-23	0.87
B3	Integration and Testing	106	207	10	5	5	-5	0.50	0	1.00

FIGURE 8.5. **Example Project Earned Value Metrics**

Take a look at the "Specifications" task in August. The project got off to a bad start—fifty-seven days of work were planned, and in fact sixty were undertaken. However, progress was slow—only forty days' worth of specifications work was actually achieved. In September, the team were more up to speed, but in October we found that we needed some additional effort to complete the specifications without affecting the overall schedule. Conversely, look at the "Reports" task in November. We planned on nineteen days of work, and indeed this was undertaken. But the task proved to be much easier than anticipated, and we made forty days of progress, finishing this task off. Finally, look at the figures for "Project Management." We don't have a measure of progress for this, so all we can say is that nineteen days were worked each month.

The Earned Value metrics for the project at this point are shown in Figure 8.5. Areas of concern are highlighted (in white in the figure and red in the Cost Model itself). There is a cost overrun for the "Usage Stats" and "Specifications" tasks and a schedule overrun for "Integration and Testing." However, the overall Estimate at Completion (*EAC*) is slightly below that planned, and the current rates of progress and productivity seem to have settled down, with *SPI* and *CPI* both greater than 1.0.

Adjusting the Model

That example assumed that I did not change my plan each month. In practice, of course, I would have needed to do so. For example, in August when I saw that progress on the Specifications had been slow, I could either have adjusted the amount of effort to be applied or lengthened the schedule. So every month (or each time period, depending on how frequently you wish to monitor the project status), the entire Cost Model must be reviewed in line with the measures of progress and cost shown up in the Earned Value metrics. This may mean a few minor adjustments, or a major overhaul of the entire model.

Both *SPI* and *CPI* are important figures to monitor, but *CPI* is the more critical. Eventually, *SPI*—the ratio of work completed to that planned—will get back to 1.0. We may have to re-plan and so may never complete all the work originally envisaged, but eventually we will complete something in accordance with the plan at that time. On the other hand, *CPI*—the ratio of actual cost to planned cost—is very difficult to recover once it drops below 1.0. We may push *SPI* back toward 1.0 by adding extra resources, but this will damage *CPI*. The only way to increase *CPI* is to focus management resources on the failing tasks or hope to recover the overall position from other tasks that complete below their planned cost.

Because I choose to evaluate Earned Value in terms of days rather than money, I cannot see if I am exceeding a task's planned cost through the utilisation of more expensive staff. In most cases, however, I can get a feel for such trends on a project-wide basis. Tracking the cash cost of each Work Package is usually not worth the effort, although it can be done.

Visualising Progress

I am not going to claim that Excel is the best tool for project tracking, and you may find it easier to use Microsoft Project or a similar tool. However, we can use facilities of Excel to graph some of the Earned Value metrics and so obtain a visualisation of trends in progress and costs.

A few years ago, during a year-long project, I maintained a historical view of the plans and metrics as the system evolved. Figure 8.6 shows the situation at the end of month five. The "Plan" is my original estimate, but *BCWS* reveals how this was revised along the way. *BCWP* shows how much actual progress has been made, and *ACWP* indicates how much time has been booked by the project team members. For the same project, Figure 8.7 shows that both *SPI* and *CPI* are healthy at month five—values over 1.0 indicate we are making good progress and have high productivity.

TRACKING ITERATIVE PROJECTS

Earned Value Management is particularly suited to iterative methods of development. Earlier, we saw that the costing of such projects should concentrate on

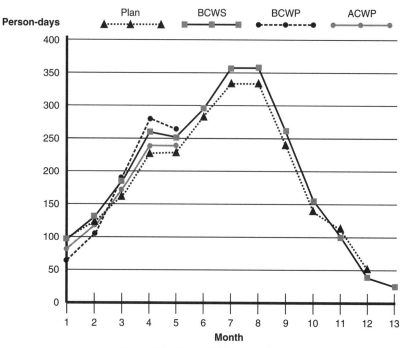

FIGURE 8.6. Earned Value Metrics

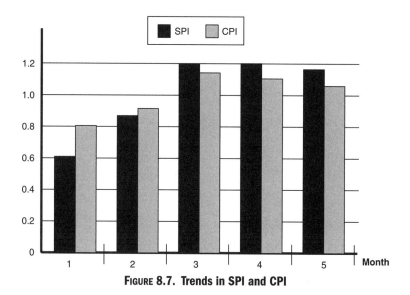

FIGURE 8.7. Trends in SPI and CPI

the next stage, with subsequent stages being estimated rather vaguely in terms of number, duration, and resource. Each iteration earns value with respect to the overall project goals. The end of a stage is the ideal point to assess the Earned Value metrics, which can then be used as a part of the planning process for the next. For example, if progress on the previous stage was slow we may set less ambitious targets, whereas if productivity was poor we may revise the team's skill sets.

TRACKING THE CRITICAL CHAIN

Absorbing Variances in the Contingency Buffers

If a contingency allowance has been made for each task, Earned Value should normally be high. When a risk strikes, the built-in contingency should be sufficient to prevent the measures of *SPI* and *CPI* dropping below 1.0. If this is not the case, there are three possibilities:

1. The contingency allowed for the risks is insufficient.
2. We have been particularly unlucky in that several risks have occurred at once.
3. Additional, unforeseen risks have occurred.

Whichever is true, the underlying reason must be discovered and the project re-planned. It could well be that the contingency allowance will need to be reviewed in line with your current view of the character and likelihood of the risks.

If we have adopted the Critical Chain technique of inserting contingency buffers into the plan, we will need frequent and accurate measures of the amount consumed from each buffer. In Figure 8.8, we have a planned a chain of four tasks with a feeding buffer of three months.

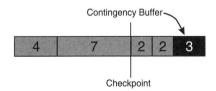

FIGURE 8.8. Example Work Package

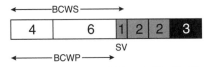

FIGURE 8.9. Earned Value at Month 11

We have reached a checkpoint at month eleven. Figure 8.9 shows that the first task in the chain completed to time, but for the second we have expended seven months of work (*BCWS*) but only achieved six months in Earned Value (*BCWP*). However, we can re-plan, as in Figure 8.10, taking the one-month Schedule Variance (*SV*) out of the contingency buffer, and still achieve the original end-date. At the next checkpoint, we will reassess all the Earned Value metrics and plan to consume more of the contingency buffer if necessary.

In that example I only measured the Schedule Variance, but Cost Variance is equally important, so we can tell if the time being booked by the team is consistent with that planned for each task. Prioritisation of the remaining work must follow the following order:

1. Chains that are eating into the Project Buffer.
2. Chains that have exhausted their Feeding Buffer, but which have not yet affected the Project Buffer.
3. Chains eating into their Feeding Buffer.
4. Chains with no Schedule Variance or Cost Variance.

Managing the Relay Race

When discussing the Critical Chain techniques, I showed how schedules could suffer from student syndrome and multitasking, and how any time saved through early completion can rarely be utilised. We want to run a project like a relay race, where each athlete strives as best they can, handing the baton on to the next—the whole team benefiting from a fast time set by one individual. Imagine if every runner in such a team was given a maximum time in which it

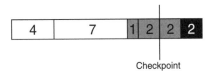

FIGURE 8.10. Re-planned Work Package

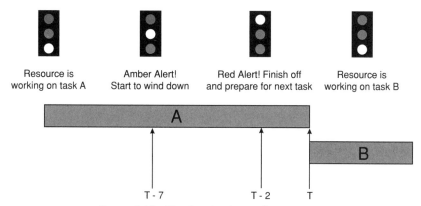

Resource is working on task A	Amber Alert! Start to wind down	Red Alert! Finish off and prepare for next task	Resource is working on task B

FIGURE 8.11. Alerting the Start of a New Task

was acceptable to complete their leg; that the earliest they could start was at a fixed moment regardless of whatever their team-mates had achieved, but that this start time could be delayed if any of the previous runners were slow; and that the team was attempting to run more than one leg at once, switching between them according to which runner was slowest. That's pretty much how we usually manage projects. In a Critical Chain development, we don't constrain teams to finish by a specified date or ask them to work on several tasks at once; we just ask them to work as fast as they can. If problems occur, there are contingency buffers to permit completion in an acceptable, if not world-record, time.

In the relay race, the runners for the next leg must be in place on the track, watching the progress of the previous athletes, so they can be ready to take the baton while already on the run. Similarly, in the project management situation, we need to provide early warnings to individuals or sub-teams that the previous steps—the prerequisites for them to start a particular task—are concluding. For example, there may be an "amber alert" at one week before completion and a "red alert" two days before, as shown in Figure 8.11.

On receiving an alert, the team scheduled to undertake the next task know when they must be ready to start on the new work. If that work is prioritised, because it is a part of the Critical Chain, they must be prepared to drop all other tasks in order to pay attention to their new assignment.

Progress tracking in such an environment is not so much an evaluation of the amount achieved as a count of the number of days to go—how long before the baton can be passed to the next team. Overall progress can be measured by the Earned Value achieved along the Critical Chain.

CHAPTER 9

Evaluating Success

Wise men profit more from fools than fools from wise men; for the wise men shun the mistakes of fools, but fools do not imitate the successes of the wise.

—*Cato the Elder*

REVIEWING THE PROJECT

"The more I practice, the luckier I get" is a remark attributed to golfer Gary Player. His point is as relevant to estimation as it is to putting. Lucky—or should I say accurate—estimates are obtained through experience. This does not just mean experience of other estimates, but experience of entire projects, both successful and unsuccessful. Instead, all we learn from history is that we learn nothing from history. A project goes bad, loses millions, produces no useful results, causes sweat and heartbreak for the team—and at the end everyone breathes a sigh of relief, and starts on the estimate for the next one. How accurate will *that* be? Well, not very. No one will want to repeat their recent unpleasant experiences, so the estimates are going to be cautious—really cautious—cautious enough so the project never starts, in fact. And as for that idiot who came up with those previous figures—well, we'd better make sure he gets nowhere near the estimation of this one.

This is the wrong use of some valuable experience. You are a better estimator after some failures. Although I have undertaken many estimates, I am still prepared to study a single subroutine to find some sign of why getting *that* one to work took ten times longer than its equally sized brothers. We need to learn from our experiences and to exploit that learning in our future projects. And the way to do that is to employ Rule 12.

> **Blindingly Obvious Rule of Estimation Number 12**
> *Hold a project post mortem.*

The post mortem review or debrief should be undertaken for all projects—those that go to plan as well as those which go badly, for there is much experience to be gleaned from both. So why are such reviews so rarely held?

- *The project changed out of all recognition* during the development, so making the original estimates redundant. But why did that happen? Were the risks foreseen? Were the changes well planned and handled?
- *It would be difficult without pointing the blame at individuals.* But the point of a post mortem review is not to assign blame, but to pool experience, to learn, and to improve.
- *Everyone is fed up with the accursed thing.* But unless you learn the lessons of this project then you will repeat the same mistakes on the next.

The sort of questions you should be asking in your post mortem review are as follows:

- Did the project meet the estimated timescales or budget? How much were we out?
- Were the desired team structures and skill sets achieved and maintained? If not, why?
- Was the list of tasks in the original estimate correct? If not what was added and removed and why? How did these tasks affect the estimated timescales and costs?
- Were the base estimates for each predicted task correct? If not, why?
- Were the assumptions that underpinned the task contingency allowances correct? If not, was the contingency sufficient? Did other task-specific events occur that were unpredicted?
- Was the Risk Analysis correct? Which risks occurred, and which did not? Were they anticipated? Were the risks detected in time? Did the risk management plan work? Was the contingency sufficient? If not, why?

- Were the capital costs and ongoing costs estimated correctly? If not, why?
- Did we ever reap the benefits predicted for the project?

It should be possible to answer these questions without personal acrimony. It is not even necessary to write anything down. Just synthesise the experience and remember it.

COLLECTING STATISTICS

In a larger organisation, you should be working on processes to formalise and improve the estimation process—creating your own checklists of risks and recording project size and effort data. This is particularly true if you want to get any value out of tools like COCOMO. I have never worked anywhere where this happens, and yet it seems almost inconceivable that organisations are prepared to cost new projects without any metrics from previous successes or failures. The ideal would be a tool that collects data such as the following:

- application area (e.g., military, financial, or communications)
- specific application (e.g., display of stock prices)
- general characteristics (e.g., database, real time, or modelling)
- specific characteristics
- technical characteristics (e.g., hardware platform, system software, middleware, database, and development tools)
- constraints (e.g., reliability and performance)
- size (e.g., lines of code, Function Points, or both)
- size breakdown between major components
- other metrics (e.g., number of database entities and transaction volumes)
- complexity assessments
- estimated effort total
- estimated effort breakdown (between project phases)
- actual effort total and breakdown
- schedule—estimated and actual
- risks (e.g., Which were identified? Which occurred? Which were not identified? What was the impact? Risk detection and management plans and their effectiveness)
- benefits—predicted and achieved
- staff roles, team structure, grades, or experience
- previous experience with the technologies used

- names of key staff
- processes used during the development
- amount of reused code, and reusable code produced by this project
- documentation produced
- project diary (e.g., key events, major changes, and milestones)
- project manager's debrief

When a new project comes along, you could enter the details that you know or can guess at, such as the application area, size, technology to be used, and so on. The database would then reveal similar projects, tell you the problems to watch out for, and whom to contact. I don't know of an application that does all this—it sounds like it needs some really modern techniques, like a neural net. But maybe someone reading this book would like to write such a tool. The cost of developing it would be . . . well, I hope that if you have read this far then you can see how that might be determined.

CHAPTER 10

Case Study

I once taught a small beginning physics class on the thirteenth floor of Hunter College in New York City. From the window we had a magnificent view of the skyscrapers of midtown Manhattan. In one of the opening sessions, I wanted to teach my students about estimates and significant figures, so I asked them to estimate the height of the Empire State Building. In a class of ten students, not one came within a factor of two of the correct answer (1472 feet with the TV tower, 1250 without). Most of the estimates were between 300 and 500 feet. One student thought 50 feet was right—a truly amazing underestimate; another thought it was a mile. It turned out that this person had actually calculated the answer, guessing 50 feet per storey, and 100 storeys or so, thus getting about 5000 feet. Where one person thought each storey was 50 feet high, another thought the whole 102-storey building was that high.

—*Douglas R. Hopfstadter*

PROJECT SUMMARY

We are a software house and have received a Request for Proposal (RFP) from Thrifty Insurance. The system they want is intended to support the administration of annuity products, mainly pensions. Its principal functions are as follows:

- **Set up a new annuity**, either from manual input or automatically from an existing quotations system. Company schemes can be established, and there are several different types of annuity product. New or augmented details are recorded in a database and confirmed to the customer by letter. Tax is an important factor—for example, each new annuity must be reported to the tax authorities.

- **Service an annuity**, maintaining details of product schemes, customers, contracts, and payment methods. Thrifty wish to set up a call centre of thirty stations that will allow customers to make telephone enquiries. All actions by call centre staff are to be recorded in an audit trail. New information may also arrive by letter. Customers are contacted every three years to ensure unnecessary payments are not being made. Some customer-requested changes must be passed to actuaries for further analysis.

- **Produce payments.** The existing quotations system undertakes the calculations, interfacing with the proposed administration system so that customers can be informed of their current position. However, the administration system must generate the actual payments by cheque or credit transfer, taking account of the relevant tax position. There is an interface to Thrifty's ledger systems. Customers entitled to more than one payment should receive these in a single amount. If the amount being paid has changed for any reason, the customer must be informed of this. Company schemes have different rules—for example, individual payslips may be produced if the company has contracted for such a service. Reports are submitted to the tax authorities and internal departments.

- **Cease payments.** This can be triggered by the death of a customer, in which case all relevant information must be collated and confirmed and the customer's final financial position determined. Any overpayments must be pursued. If the annuity is to continue to be paid to a dependent, their details must be collected and further calculations made. Alternatively, the annuity may have reached the end of its contracted term, in which case the customer is informed by letter. Finally, a customer may request commutation (transfer to a single lump-sum payment), which implies various payment and tax processes.

- **Process year-end tasks.** These mainly consist of additional reports to the tax authorities and internal departments. The former may change any of the factors affecting tax calculations and inform Thrifty of customers' tax codes.

The following information is also relevant to the estimate:

- The system will be developed at our offices and then installed at Thrifty for acceptance and cutover. A period of parallel running with existing systems will be needed.
- We will be supplying and installing all the new hardware for the system and will be responsible for all licences for third-party system software.
- We will be training the users of the system—operators and call centre staff—and supplying appropriate documentation.
- We will be supporting the system for three months after it goes into live use.
- We will not be responsible for any ongoing costs.
- We will be adopting a "waterfall" development life cycle.
- Thrifty have imposed standards for the hardware, operating system, database management system, transaction processing middleware, programming language, networking, workflow, word processing, and system management software.
- The currency for all costs is pounds sterling (GBP).

This is a large project, and details of the required functionality are far from clear. For example, the facilities available at the call centre terminals are only implied, not specified by the RFP. Despite this, Thrifty want a fixed-price quotation for the entire system, up to and including the support phase.

TECHNICAL TASKS

Some of the sheets in the Cost Model for this project are too large to be printed in their entirety. However, the complete model can be found on the CD included with this book. The Task List for the technical tasks is shown in Figure 10.1, along with my estimates for duration and task contingency.

We are already beginning to get a feel for the size of the project. Using my rules of thumb, we are talking about $2882 \times 4 = 11,528$ person-days, or around 600 person-months, implying a team of around twenty-five for two years. If Thrifty Insurance is planning to be operating the new system after *one* year, I am now in a position to ring some warning bells. There are no obvious way in which the development can be divided into autonomous subprojects; everything uses a common database, and the interdependencies are complex. And we already have a high risk—27.8 percent before we have even considered project-wide factors. I'm not saying that a fifty-person team for one year would be impossible, but it would be an immensely risky undertaking for an already risky project.

Ref	Task	Base Days	Task Cont. %	Task Cont. Days	Notes
A	**Annuity New Business Setup**				
A1	Enter/Validate new/augmented data				Interfaces to Quotations system covered elsewhere
A1.1	Unique Ids	3	15%	3	Annuitant and scheme/policy
A1.2	Personal pensioner details	5	15%	6	App. 20 fields
A1.3	Corporate/trustee details	5	15%	6	App. 20 fields
A1.4	Previous contract details	1	15%	1	App. 5 fields
A1.5	Contract & benefit structure details	30	15%	35	App. 10 types x 30 fields
A1.6	Payment details	15	15%	17	App. 10 types x 10 fields
A1.7	Escalation details	7	15%	8	App. 5 types x 5 fields
A1.8	Step pension details	5	15%	6	App. 3 types x 5 fields
A1.9	Inland revenue limits	7	15%	8	App. 30 fields
A1.10	Lump sum details	4	15%	5	App. 10 fields
A1.11	Split details	4	15%	5	App. 10 fields
A1.12	Valuation details	5	40%	7	App. 20 fields. Needs a report?
A1.13	Static data & cross checks	15	20%	18	Where needed above
A1.14	Validation against external databases	30	30%	39	Clients, products, schemes, tax, banks
A2	Set up new record	15	20%	18	
A3	Link with other annuities	10	15%	12	One payment
A4	Pass to other relevant Trusty systems	20	50%	30	Details vague, reconcile data records?
A5	Auto generation of info to Inland Revenue	15	20%	18	Output by listing or EDI
A6	Other documentation	20	30%	26	Customer, internal, trustees
A7	New business statistics	20	30%	26	Actuarial, sales & marketing, campaign info.
A8	Reverse a new case	5	20%	6	Before 1st payment made
A9	Handle cooling-off period	5	50%	8	What does system need to do?
A10	Extra hassle for augmentations to existing policies	15	15%	17	
B	**Annuity Administration**				
B1	General enquiries	20	15%	23	On scheme no, customer name, number
B2	Updates	50	20%	60	Mainly as for initial entry
B3	Actuarially sensitive info	10	75%	18	Detect and Report?
B4	Trigger manual investigation	5	50%	8	Criteria?
B5	Control updates to financial info	5	20%	6	Needs confirmation that payment received
B6	Search for related annuities	2	15%	2	
B7	Multi-annuity changes	20	20%	24	
B8	Suspend/resume payments	3	15%	3	By scheme, annuity or annuitant
B9	Lost policy holder	10	20%	12	Suspend, pay into holding account
B10	Bankrupcy and Insolvency cases	5	20%	6	
B11	Reverse split	5	20%	6	
B12	One-off payments	5	20%	6	
B13	Diary	10	15%	12	Setup and display
B13.1	Benefit changes	2	15%	2	
B13.2	Recommencements	2	15%	2	
B13.3	Cert. Of Entitlement	2	15%	2	
B13.4	Amendment	3	15%	3	
B13.5	Enact Events	3	15%	3	
B14	Issue Cert. Of Continuing Entitlement	3	15%	3	
B15	Administer CoCE	20	20%	24	

FIGURE 10.1. Case Study Task List

C	Payment Control				
C1	Calculate and pay first instalment	15	20%	18	Including tax calculation
C2	Calc & pay subsequent instalments	10	20%	12	Ditto
C3	Calc & pay arrears	10	20%	12	Ditto
C4	Monitor against IR payment limits	5	15%	6	
C5	Pay gross instalments to trustees	10	15%	12	Print schedule of individual payments
C6	Pay step pensions	10	15%	12	
C7	Admin and provision of tax info				
C7.1	Schedule D	8	15%	9	
C7.2	Schedule E	8	15%	9	
C7.3	PLA	5	15%	6	
C7.4	Isle of Man	5	15%	6	
C7.5	Guernsey	5	15%	6	
C7.6	Jersey	5	15%	6	
C8	Payments interface	50	20%	60	Various formats, different company accounts
C9	Reclaim under reassurance arrangements	30	100%	60	Very unclear
C10	Non-insured payments	15	40%	21	Report?
C11	Combine payments	10	20%	12	If several to same annuitant
C12	Letters/Advice				
C12.1	Initial letter	3	15%	3	
C12.2	First Payment letter	3	15%	3	
C12.3	Payment Slip	3	15%	3	
C12.4	Payment Advice Notice	10	25%	13	If any changes
C13	Repayment of over-deducted tax	5	15%	6	
C14	Exception payments	5	15%	6	
C15	Payments resulting from amendments	5	15%	6	
C16	Record and recover over-payment	8	15%	9	
C17	Process returned payments	5	15%	6	
C18	Record payment status	5	15%	6	
C19	Administer payment of reimbursed pension	25	15%	29	See B&W breakdown
C20	Accrue tax due to IR	10	15%	12	
C21	Pay tax to IR	15	15%	17	
C22	Payment timetables/immediate	12	15%	14	
C23	Reasonableness checks	20	50%	30	Vague
C24	Reminders of uncashed cheques	5	15%	6	
C25	Cancel payment	3	15%	3	Batch or individual

D	Payment Cessation				
D1	Capture data on death	40	20%	48	May need a cycle of correspondence
D2	Cease payment	4	15%	5	
D3	Manual cease payment	2	15%	2	
D4	Find associated annuities and cease	10	20%	12	
D5	Calculate overpayments	30	25%	38	Last payment, unexpired guarantees, proportonate
D6	Calculate benefits/lump sums	20	25%	25	
D7	Produce documentation	30	25%	38	Correspondence, P45
D8	Process recovery of overpayment	20	25%	25	
D9	Commence spouse/dependant payment	20	25%	25	Commutate if <£260 pa
D10	Complete death processing	10	15%	12	Lump sum, final doc, close record
D11	Cease payment during life of annuity	20	20%	24	Natural cessation, issue correspondence
D12	Auto cease fixed term annuity payments	5	20%	6	Issue letter
D13	Commutations	30	25%	38	
D14	Record surrender value	10	20%	12	Surrenders, commutations, full/partial
D15	Reports to IR or internal	20	50%	30	None mentioned but there must be some

E	End-Year Processing				
E1	Calculate tax deductions				
E1.1	P14/P35	15	20%	18	
E1.2	Foreign Islands	15	20%	18	
E1.3	Balance	15	20%	18	
E2	Inform pensioner or trustee of tax				
E2.2	P60	10	20%	12	
E2.3	Schedule D	10	20%	12	
E2.4	PLA Certificate	10	20%	12	
E2.5	Suppress production	2	15%	2	
E3	End of year fiscal procedures	30	50%	45	Vague
E4	Record/recreate historical data	20	25%	25	
E5	Produce end of year reports	30	50%	45	Vague
E6	Produce DTI/CMI Information	40	50%	60	Vague

Figure **10.1.** *(continued)*

F	Reports and Letters				
F1	Standard reports	210	20%	252	70 in all, allegedly not much calculation
F2	Ad hoc reports	20	25%	25	Front end to Crystal
F3	Standard letters	140	20%	168	70 letters, claims, advice etc. Word templates
F4	Reproduce any document	10	15%	12	Legal need to recreate letters
G	Other Requirements				
G1	Extract actuarial data				
G1.1	Individual	10	20%	12	
G1.2	Scheme	10	20%	12	
G1.3	Ad Hoc	10	20%	12	
G1.4	SIB Review	10	20%	12	
G2	Extract Finance Systems data				
G2.1	Annuity movements	10	20%	12	
G2.2	Movement reconciliation	10	20%	12	
G2.3	Payment reconciliation	10	20%	12	
G2.4	Returned payments	10	20%	12	
G2.5	BACS Return payments	10	20%	12	
G2.6	Overpayments	10	20%	12	
G2.7	Suspended cases	10	20%	12	
G2.8	Reimbused pensions	10	20%	12	
G2.9	Tax payment	10	20%	12	
H	Interfaces				
H1	Quote systems	40	50%	60	Info on all these is poor
H2	Actuarial	20	50%	30	
H3	UK Statutory companies	30	50%	45	
H4	Finance	20	50%	30	
H5	Party	30	50%	45	
H6	DSS	30	50%	45	
H7	Tax and legislative bodies	40	50%	60	
H8	BACS	30	20%	36	
H9	Cheque production	15	50%	23	
H10	Bulk Output	15	50%	23	
H11	Scheme admin	15	50%	23	
H12	Marketing	15	50%	23	
H13	Scheme valuation	15	50%	23	
H14	Roll forward/back	50	30%	65	Recovery for all interfaces above
I	Miscellaneous				
I1	Audit Trail	20	15%	23	And ability to view/search
I2	Archive	4	15%	5	
I3	Backup/restore database	1	15%	1	Standard
I4	Logon/logoff, user privileges	10	15%	12	Assume nothing special
I5	Usability	15	20%	18	Help, navigation
I6	Data Processing Act compliance report	2	15%	2	
J	Operations				
J1	Software distribution	2	15%	2	
J2	Recovery	8	15%	9	Hardware, network, workstations
J3	Batch invocation & status	15	15%	17	
J4	System status	8	15%	9	
J5	Print status	8	20%	10	
J6	Interfaces status	15	15%	17	
J7	Scheduling	15	15%	17	Capability to adjust for delays

Base Total	2255	Days	
Task Contingency	27.8%	627	
Total with Task Contingency		2882	

FIGURE **10.1.** *(continued)*

OVERHEAD TASKS

I can now plan my project timescale. Because we are following a waterfall life-cycle, I can lay out the different phases and put an approximate duration on each, as shown in Table 10.1.

TABLE 10.1. Case Study Project Phases	
Phase	Project Months
Functional Specification (including user interfaces and workflows)	1–5
Technical Specification (including database design)	3–8
Code and unit test	8–14
Integration test (including test specifications)	11–17
System test (including test specifications)	16–20
Acceptance test (to agreed specifications)	20–23
Installation	21–22
Parallel Running	23–26
Support	27–29

Some phases can overlap, and I have been generous with the "up-front" tasks because I can see that there is much specification work to do. Because I have this outline plan, I'll postpone the construction of the detailed Task Plan until I have undertaken the estimates for the overhead tasks. These are shown in Figure 10.2.

The grand total is looking to be greater than my rule of thumb estimate, especially as we haven't yet added any project-wide contingency. This may suggest that the overall timeframe should be extended, which in turn would increase the estimates for project management overheads in section Q. However, our sales staff have told me that unless we can plan to get the system is up and running at Thrifty's offices within two years, we will not be considered for the contract. So I'm going to stick to this limit and satisfy any remaining effort

Ref	Task	Base Days	Task Cont. %	Days	Notes
K	**Functional Specifications**				
K1	Business Analysis	80	15%	92	4 x 1 month
K2	Workflows	30	15%	35	
K3	Functional Specifications				
K3.1	Annuities and Payments	160	15%	184	4 x 2 months
K3.2	Reports, Letters, Advice	100	15%	115	Includes a style guide. Approx 150 docs
K3.3	Interfaces	60	25%	75	Approx 15
K3.4	Operations	40	20%	48	
K3.5	Other	30	15%	35	
K4	Reviews and modifications	60	50%	90	of FS. Internal and customer
K5	Database Logical Design	75	20%	90	Janet has figures for likely database effort
K6	Screen prototypes				VB, can carry into implementation
K6.1	Style guide	30	30%	39	Inc reviews
K6.2	First cut	120	15%	138	Approx 40 screens
K6.3	Review/modify	40	50%	60	Internal and customer

FIGURE 10.2. Case Study Overhead Tasks

L	Technical Specifications				
L1	Overall Design	160	20%	192	4 x 2 months
L2	Detailed Analysis				
L3	Annuities and Payments	160	20%	192	4 x 2 months
L3.1	Screens	40	15%	46	40 x 1
L3.2	Reports, Letters, Advice	75	15%	86	150 x 0.5
L3.3	Interfaces	60	25%	75	Approx 15
L3.4	Operations	40	15%	46	
L4	Walkthroughs, Reviews, and modifications	60	20%	72	Internal only
L5	Database Physical Design	100	20%	120	Janet has figures for likely database effort
L6	Database design maintenance	80	20%	96	Ditto

M	Hardware & System Software				
M1	Overall Architecture	40	20%	48	
M2	Performance & Sizing model	30	15%	35	Estimate from Brian
M3	Equipment List	20	15%	23	
M4	Sourcing and ordering	20	15%	23	
M5	Configure development environment	80	25%	100	
M6	Development system management	400	5%	420	20 months x 1
M7	Deinstall and reconfigure at customer site	80	100%	160	Interfacing to other systems
M8	On-site system management	240	10%	264	6 months x 2

N	Testing				
N1	Integration Test specification	60	15%	69	Including review
N2	Integration Tests	300	15%	345	And fix
N3	System Test specification	60	15%	69	Including review
N4	System Tests	200	15%	230	And fix
N5	Acceptance Test Specification	80	15%	92	Including internal review
N6	Agree Acceptance Test Specification	40	50%	60	With customer. And modify
N7	Dry run	150	15%	173	Internal. With fixes
N8	Customer acceptance	150	50%	225	With fixes
N9	Test Data	80	20%	96	Establish and maintain
N10	Test harnesses	80	25%	100	Emulation of external interfaces

O	Rollout and Training				
O1	Rollout Plans	25	30%	33	Including review with customer
O2	Populate Database	100	25%	125	Janet has looked at this
O3	Interfaces testing	40	50%	60	May need to meet regulatory requirements
O4	Parallel Running	360	25%	450	3 months x 6
O5	Admin Clerk Training				
O5.1	Prepare Course	60	15%	69	
O5.2	Dry Run	3	15%	3	
O5.3	Run Course	12	15%	14	3 days, run twice x 2 people
O6	Operator training				
O6.1	Prepare Course	40	15%	46	
O6.2	Dry Run	2	15%	2	
O6.3	Run Course	4	15%	5	2 days, run once x 2 people

P	Documentation				
P1	Help text	40	15%	46	40 screens
P2	Admin Clerk Manuals	70	25%	88	Agree with user reps
P3	Operator Manuals	40	15%	46	Plus some third party stuff
P4	Design specifications				Assume up to data tech specs sufficient

Q	Project Office & Overheads				
Q1	Project Manager	480		480	1 x 24 m
Q2	Technical Manager	480		480	1 x 24 m
Q3	Team Leaders				Assume 6 x 24 months
Q3.1	Pre-C&UT				PM & TM sufficient
Q3.2	C&UT	1440		1440	Assume 6 x 12m
Q3.3	Post C&UT	171		171	Assume 1 x 9m
Q4	QA	40	15%	46	Assume 2 inspections x 10 days + fixes
Q5	System management				Already counted in Section M
Q6	Librarian/Project secretary	240		240	1 x 12m
Q7	Familiarisation	600		600	30 x 1m
Q8	Project overheads	300		300	Meetings, walkthroughs, presentations

Base Total	10512	Days		
Task Contingency		15.0%	1572	
Total with Task Contingency			12084	

FIGURE 10.2. *(continued)*

requirements by adding extra labour—unless I start to get worried about the overall team size exceeding that mandated by Rule 10. Because I am now firmly committed to a two-year timeframe, I have decided not to allow any contingency for most of the "Project Office" tasks, which accounts for why the total amount of task contingency has fallen to 15 percent. Instead, I will cater for potential project overruns in the Risk Analysis.

RISK ANALYSIS

I will still postpone the construction of the Task Plan and turn to the project-wide risks. Many of the factors we are most worried about have already been allocated a large amount of risk in the task estimates—the time it will take to get approvals from the client, poor specifications of the interfaces, and on-site installation problems, for example. In discussion with the proposal team, the Risk Analysis emerged as shown in Figure 10.3.

As you can see, we weren't able to find many project-wide risks, and many of these have been assessed in terms of cash rather than days. Going back to my task estimates, I only need a project contingency of 5.63 percent to account for this, the totals ending as shown in Figure 10.4.

RISK NUMBER	1

Definition

Risk	There may be implied functionality not mentioned in the RFP, which Thrifty would expect us to know.
Cause	We have not undertaken any work in the area of annuity payments before.

Management

Prevention	We are recruiting for expertise in this area, but this will be after the proposal has been sent. May be a chance of further price negotiation if we are selected.
Trigger	Initial analysis work should show up problems. Thrifty will sign off the Functional Spec.
Plan	Review estimate after initial analysis, and after functional spec signoff.
Owner	Mary Spencer

Assessment

Probability	H	Detection	L	Impact	H	Overall	54%

Contingency Allowance

Method	Additional 10% of project time. Will affect analysis, code, test, and overheads. Unlikely to affect hardware costs. Extra on-site costs negligible.

Maximum Days	1208.4		Weighted Days	647
Maximum Cost (GBP)			Weighted Cost	

FIGURE 10.3. Case Study Risk Analysis

RISK NUMBER	2				
Definition					
Risk	Unfamiliarity with the EZ programming language.				
Cause	Thrifty use this horror for all their systems.				
Management					
Prevention	EZ is supposed to be easy if you know C++. There is expertise available in the contract market.				
Trigger	Feedback from team leaders.				
Plan	We have some staff already at Thrifty, who may become available. Training courses take 3 days (outside of a specific project budget).				
Owner	Mike Jones				
Assessment					
Probability	L	Detection L	Impact M	Overall	18%
Contingency Allowance					
Method	Assume 10% of the code (2882 days) must be written by contractors at £100 a day above our rates.				
Maximum Days				**Weighted Days**	
Maximum Cost (GBP)	28820			**Weighted Cost**	5143

RISK NUMBER	3				
Definition					
Risk	Additional performance and resiliance requirements will emerge.				
Cause	Requirements vague in RFP.				
Management					
Prevention	Proposal will make clear what we are assuming.				
Trigger	Initial discussions after award of contract.				
Plan	Given the vagueness of the requirement, it seems unliey we can be held liable for additional needs. However, our performance model may be wrong.				
Owner	Brian Kingsley				
Assessment					
Probability	L	Detection L	Impact M	Overall	18%
Contingency Allowance					
Method	Allow £12000 to upgrade to next size of processor. Capacity should not be an issue.				
Maximum Days				**Weighted Days**	
Maximum Cost (GBP)	12000			**Weighted Cost**	2143

FIGURE 10.3. *(continued)*

TASK PLAN

Now I can turn my attention to the Task Plan, using the estimates with their full contingency allowance. The result is partly shown in Figure 10.5.

To prepare this plan, I needed to take a view on which activities could run in parallel, and which had to precede others. I could have devoted some effort

RISK NUMBER 4

Definition
Risk: Cannot form on-site team.

Cause: No one wants to work in Borsetshire (previous requirement for 21 people yielded 3, and they are already there).

Management
Prevention: Build team spirit so people want to complete the job.

Trigger: Insufficient volunteers by month 18.

Plan: Determine team by month 18. If not enough can be found, increase allowances. If that doesn't work, recruit internally or externally.

Owner: Mary Spencer

Assessment
Probability: M   Detection: L   Impact: M   Overall: 25%

Contingency Allowance
Method: Increase allowances to max of £100 per day. 6 people x 6 months. This would be more than enough to cover the training of additional internal or external people.

Maximum Days
Maximum Cost (GBP): 72000   Weighted Days / Weighted Cost: 18000

RISK NUMBER 5

Definition
Risk: Requirements changing during project duration.

Cause: Project is a part of a general re-engineering/IT strategy. This may cause impacts small and great.

Management
Prevention: Change control on agreed functional spec. Changes will still need to be assessed and will disrupt.

Trigger: Changes impacting on project management or implementation team.

Plan: Normal change control. We have a hand in the overall strategy so can try to insulate this project. As a last resort we can deploy a change control manager.

Owner: Mary Spencer

Assessment
Probability: L   Detection: L   Impact: M   Overall: 18%

Contingency Allowance
Method: Assume a change control manager. 1year @ £1000 pd.

Maximum Days
Maximum Cost (GBP): 240000   Weighted Days / Weighted Cost: 42857

FIGURE 10.3. *(continued)*

to sorting out a logical ordering for the technical tasks, but that wouldn't help in deriving a price, so I'll leave the construction of the detailed schedule to the Project Manager. Instead, I have assigned the tasks to give a reasonably smooth staffing profile—starting with fourteen, peaking at thirty-nine, and ramping down to a single person in support. The peak team size is high, but not too high with respect to Rule 10, as we have an average team size of twenty-three over a

RISK NUMBER   6

Definition

Risk — Getting bogged down in negotiations over agreeing documents, payments, changes etc.

Cause — This is the first fixed price job we will have done for Thrifty. They are notoriously picky.

Management

Prevention — Close contact with senior management/sales to get early warning of potential disputes.

Trigger — Agreement timescales being exceeded. Payments late.

Plan — Task contingency has been increased for some items. They need this system so we can show them the effect that being over-fussy will have on the chances of success.

Owner — Mary Spencer

Assessment

Probability   M   Detection   M   Impact   M   Overall   32%

Contingency Allowance

Method — Allow 100 extra days for hassle. Late payments can be handled by usual procedures.

Maximum Days   100   **Weighted Days**   32
Maximum Cost (GBP)   **Weighted Cost**

Risks Estimated in Terms of Days   679
Risks Estimated in Terms of Cost (GBP)   68143

FIGURE 10.3. *(continued)*

twenty-nine-month project. The plan shows that it is just about possible to get the system ready for parallel running at Thrifty's offices within two years, even by making an allowance for all the risks we can think of.

STAFF COSTS

We can now turn our attention to the Staff Plan, part of which is shown in Figure 10.6. At this stage, I don't know the names of any team members, so I have removed that column. However, I have a Rate Book that allows me to allocate an appropriate daily rate for each staff role.

I have not paid too much attention to continuity of staff throughout the project, for example, it is probable (and indeed preferable) that the business analysts who undertake the functional specifications are also members of the

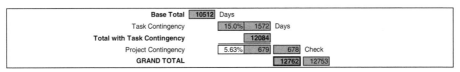

Base Total   10512   Days
Task Contingency   15.0%   1572   Days
Total with Task Contingency   12084
Project Contingency   5.63%   679   678   Check
GRAND TOTAL   12762   12753

FIGURE 10.4. Case Study Totals with Project-Wide Contingency

Ref	Task	Aug-02	Sep-02		Feb-03	Mar-03	Apr-03		Nov-04	Dec-04
	Staff Profile	13.8	21.3		33.5	37.3	39.5		2.3	1.3
	Total	262	404		637	709	750		43	24
A	**Annuity New Business Setup**									
A1	Enter/Validate new/augmented data									
A1.1	Unique Ids					3				
A1.2	Personal pensioner details					6				
A1.3	Corporate/trustee details					6				
A1.4	Previous contract details					1				
A1.5	Contract & benefit structure details					37				
A1.6	Payment details						18			
A1.7	Escalation details						8			
A1.8	Step pension details						6			
A1.9	Inland revenue limits						8			
A1.10	Lump sum details						5			
A1.11	Split details						5			
A1.12	Valuation details						7			
Q	**Project Office & Overheads**									
Q1	Project Manager	19	19		19	19	19			
Q2	Technical Manager	19	19		19	19	19			
Q3	Team Leaders									
Q3.1	Pre-C&UT									
Q3.2	C&UT					133	133			
Q3.3	Post C&UT								19	
Q4	QA									
Q5	System management									
Q6	Librarian/Project secretary						19			
Q7	Familiarisation	38	38		95	76	38			
Q8	Project overheads	5	5		10	10	10		5	5

FIGURE **10.5. Case Study Task Plan**

development teams. However, such issues will not affect the price too much; I can apply typical rates for each project role rather than worry about whether specific people have the right mix of skills. If we win the contract to develop this project, we will need to allocate suitable staff for each role and then determine the set of roles each one is qualified to fill. This may affect the cost, but so long as I have been careful not to assign an excessive amount of work to junior roles, we should not be too far out.

You may be surprised how much the project seems to cost—£14m, and we have not added our capital costs or profit margin yet. I was not *too* surprised, because I have another rule of thumb—that the average rate for staff in my organisation is £1,000 per day. So I could deduce a cost of at least £12m from the Task Plan. In fact, the average staff cost for this project is £1,111 per day, as shown in Figure 10.6; maybe I need to update my rule of thumb.

Because the project crosses year-boundaries, we would usually need to consider a possible increase in staff rates. The Cost Model has a facility to incorporate such rises, but in this case we have an agreement with Thrifty Insurance that freezes our rates until 2005, so I do not need to apply any inflation allowance for this project.

Capital Costs

Now we turn to the list of capital costs. The technical team has undertaken a preliminary sizing so we can determine the capacities of the equipment we intend to deploy. Quotations for supply and installation of this hardware have been obtained from our usual suppliers.

We also need to consider the cost of moving our team on site for the final phases of acceptance and parallel running. Here I have used numbers from the Staff Plan to determine the number of days that our team will be deployed at Thrifty's offices. I can then use standard rates to assess the amount we are going to need for their accommodation and expenses. The resulting Capital Costs sheet is shown in Figure 10.7.

Role	Days	Rate	GBP	Aug-02	Sep-02	Oct-02	Nov-04	Dec-04
Project Manager	551	1800	991800	19	19	19	19	19
Technical Manager	513	1800	923400	19	19	19		
Business Analysis Consultant	95	2500	237500	19	19	19		
Senior Analyst/Designer 1	95	1300	123500	19	19	19		
Senior Analyst/Designer 2	76	1300	98800	19	19	19		
Senior Analyst/Designer 3	38	1300	49400		19	19		
Senior Analyst/Designer 4	57	1300	74100		19	19		
Junior Analyst/Designer 1	95	900	85500	19	19	19		
Junior Analyst/Designer 2	76	900	68400		19	19		
Junior Analyst/Designer 3	57	900	51300		19	19		
Junior Analyst/Designer 4	76	900	68400	19	19	19		
Junior Analyst/Designer 5	76	900	68400	19	19	19		
Trainee Analyst 1	76	600	45600		19	19		
Trainee Analyst 2	57	600	34200		19	19		
Trainee Analyst 3	76	600	45600	19	19	19		
Architect/System Designer	57	2000	114000	19	19	19		
Performance Analyst	3 8	2000	76000	19	19			
User Interface Consultant	57	1300	74100			19		
Senior UI Analyst	95	1000	95000	19	19	19		
Junior UI Analyst	76	850	64600		19	19		
Senior Database Designer	252	1500	378000	19	19	19		
Junior Database Designer	76	1000	76000					
System Maintenance Team Leader	542	1300	704600	10	19	19	19	19
System Maintenance Engineer 1	285	800	228000		19			
System Maintenance Engineer 2	133	800	106400					
System Maintenance Engineer 3	57	800	45600					
System Maintenance Engineer 4	19	800	15200					
Development Team A Leader	323	1500	484500			19		
Senior Programmer/Analyst 1	285	1300	370500			19		
Senior Programmer/Analyst 2	190	1300	247000					
Junior Programmer/Analyst 1	266	900	239400					
Junior Programmer/Analyst 2	152	900	136800					
Trainee Programmer/Analyst 1	209	600	125400					
Trainee Programmer/Analyst 2	152	600	91200					
Trainee Programmer/Analyst 3	114	600	68400					
Trainee Programmer/Analyst 4	76	600	45600					
Development Team B Leader	247	1500	370500			19		
Senior Programmer/Analyst 1	209	1300	271700					
Senior Programmer/Analyst 2	190	1300	247000					
Junior Programmer/Analyst 1	152	900	136800					
Junior Programmer/Analyst 2	190	900	171000					
Trainee Programmer/Analyst 1	152	600	91200					
Trainee Programmer/Analyst 2	152	600	91200					
Trainee Programmer/Analyst 3	133	600	79800					
Trainee Programmer/Analyst 4	76	600	45600					

Figure 10.6. Case Study Staff Plan

Role	Total Days	Average Rate	Cost (GBP)		
Development Team C Leader	304	1500	456000		
Senior Programmer/Analyst 1	266	1300	345800		
Senior Programmer/Analyst 2	171	1300	222300		
Junior Programmer/Analyst 1	152	900	136800		
Junior Programmer/Analyst 2	247	900	222300		
Trainee Programmer/Analyst 1	209	600	125400		
Trainee Programmer/Analyst 2	114	600	68400		
Trainee Programmer/Analyst 3	57	600	34200		
Development Team D Leader	190	1500	285000		
Senior Programmer/Analyst 1	190	1300	247000		
Senior Programmer/Analyst 2	171	1300	222300		
Junior Programmer/Analyst 1	114	900	102600		
Junior Programmer/Analyst 2	152	900	136800		
Trainee Programmer/Analyst 1	152	600	91200		
Trainee Programmer/Analyst 2	133	600	79800		
Trainee Programmer/Analyst 3	19	600	11400		
Rollout/Cutover Team Leader	190	1500	285000		19
Senior Rollout Team Member 1	152	1300	197600		
Senior Rollout Team Member 1	152	1300	197600		
Junior Rollout Team Member 1	133	900	119700		
Junior Rollout Team Member 2	95	900	85500		
Junior Rollout Team Member 3	57	900	51300		
Trainee Rollout Team Member 1	57	600	34200		
Trainee Rollout Team Member 2	19	600	11400		
Trainee Rollout Team Member 3	19	600	11400		
Test Team Leader	304	1500	456000		
Tester 1	304	800	243200		
Tester 2	247	800	197600		
Tester 3	209	800	167200		
Tester 4	190	800	152000		
Tester 5	171	800	136800		
Tester 6	76	800	60800		
Tester 7	38	800	30400		
Technical Writing Team Leader	152	1500	228000		
Technical Writer	114	600	68400		
Training Team Leader	95	1500	142500		
Trainer	76	900	68400		
QA Team	50	1800	90000	25	
Secretarial Support	247	400	98800		

	Total Days	Average Rate	Cost (GBP)		Staff Profile	13.5	21	26.3		3	2
	12757	1111	14178100		Total Days	257	399	500		57	38
Check	12762				Check	262	404	505		43	24

FIGURE 10.6. *(continued)*

In this sheet, I have incorporated the elements from the Risk Analysis that were assessed in terms of cost, a total of £68,143. This yielded a project-wide contingency of 8.65 percent to be added to the capital cost figures.

This is a fixed-price development, so all the capital costs will be included in those for the initial project development. Thrifty will be responsible for accounting for depreciation. The allocation of the capital costs is shown in Figure 10.8.

I used the figures from the Staff Plan to help in the calculation of the on-site costs—the monthly totals are proportional to the number of staff working on the project at the time. The installation/de-installation costs have been

Base Total	710798	

Item Contingency	10.8%	76915	GBP
Total with Item Contingency		787713	
Project Contingency	8.65%	68143	68138

Total Capital Costs (GBP)	855851

Ref	Item	Supplier	Notes	Cost (GBP)	Qty.	Base Cost	Item Cont %	GBP	Total (GBP)
1	Development and target hardware	Pukka Systems	See Quotation #QL83726	276272	1	276272	5%	290086	315178
2	Installation/deinstallation at Hackitout offices.	Flybynight Logistics	See Quotation 36335DS	13272	1	13272	5%	13935.6	15141
3	System software, including OS licences, development environment, TP monitor, system monitor etc.	Jubbly Software	See Quotation HGTR867. May need additional licences if development team increases	98654	1	98654	15%	113452	123266
4	On-site expenses (hotels, meals, travel).		Total Days on Site * Onsite Expenses Allowance	209000	1	209000	15%	240350	261140
5	On-site allowances.		Total Days on Site * Onsite Personal Allowance	83600	1	83600	15%	96140	104456
6	Misc expenses - socials, travel, meals etc.			25000	1	25000	15%	28750	31237
7	Consumables			5000	1	5000		5000	5433

FIGURE 10.7. Case Study Capital Costs List

assigned as one-third for the development system installation, and two-thirds for the transfer to Thrifty's offices. Miscellaneous expenses and the cost of consumables are distributed equally throughout the development stage of the project.

We will be ordering the development system during the first month and expect to have it delivered and installed soon after we have issued the order. However, the bills for it won't arrive—or be paid—until later, so the costs have been assigned to month three.

						Included in Project Costs				Oct-04	Nov-04	Dec-04
Ref	Item	Total (GBP)	Check	Depreciate From	Years	Aug-02	Sep-02	Oct-02		33236	24927	16618
						1527	1527	445018				
1	Development and target hardware	315178	315178					315178				
2	Installation/deinstallation at Hackitout offices.	15141	15141					5047				
3	System software, including OS licences, development environment, TP monitor, system monitor etc.	123266	123266					123266				
4	On-site expenses (hotels, meals, travel).	261140	261140							23740	17805	11870
5	On-site allowances.	104456	104456							9496	7122	4748
6	Misc expenses - socials, travel, meals etc.	31237	31224			1301	1301	1301				
7	Consumables	5433	5424			226	226	226				

FIGURE 10.8. Case Study Capital Costs Distribution

COST SUMMARY Thrifty Insurance - Annuities Administration System				
	Total (GBP)	**2002**	**2003**	**2004**
Staff Costs	14178100	2632500	8020000	3525600
Capital Costs	855829	451126	18324	386379
Total Initial Cost	**15033929**	3083626	8038324	3911979
Ongoing Costs				
Total Project Cost	**15033929**	3083626	8038324	3911979

FIGURE 10.9. Case Study Cost Summary

SUMMARY

We can now examine the Cost Summary shown in Figure 10.9 to see the total cost of the project, including the capital costs.

CASHFLOW

Having estimated a cost of around £15m for the project, the estimation team undertook a review with the sales department and senior management. It was decided that we should quote a fixed price of £20m to Thrifty Insurance. The sales people thought this would be acceptable, so long as we felt confident about the overall delivery schedule. It was also decided that the best payment terms we could quote were £5m at the start of the project, £5m at the end of month twelve, £5m when the on-site tests started around month twenty-two, and the final £5m when the parallel running period was complete. Finally, the senior management wanted to see the cost of borrowed or deposited money reflected in the Cost Model, so that a realistic profit figure could be assessed. Thrifty usually paid their bills within three months of presentation, and this also needed to be taken into account. Putting all this information into the Cashflow sheet yielded Figure 10.10.

Instead of entering a mark-up percentage, I entered our final price of £20m under "Income" and let the spreadsheet work out the resulting margin of 21.24 percent.

I have been told that we are charged 2 percent on the total outstanding amount borrowed every month, but we are paid 1 percent on the total we are in credit. These percentages are applied to the gross cashflow for each month, yielding a total of £840,539 in interest charges and £123,057 in interest earned. These amounts are then used to calculate the net cashflow, with the interest taken into account.

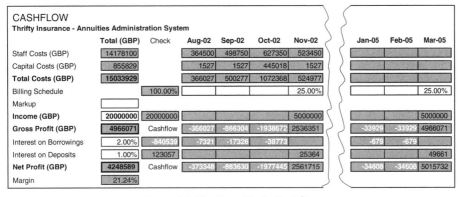

FIGURE **10.10. Case Study Cashflow**

DIAGRAMS

Here I have chosen to produce some diagrams for the staff profile (Figure 10.11) and the cashflow (Figure 10.12).

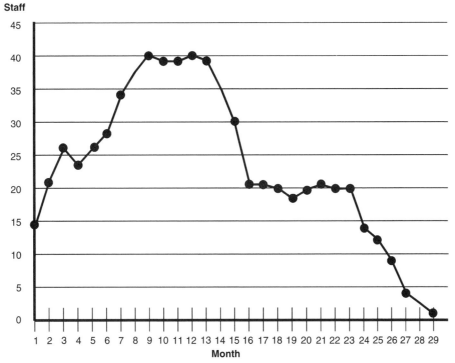

FIGURE **10.11. Case Study Staff Profile**

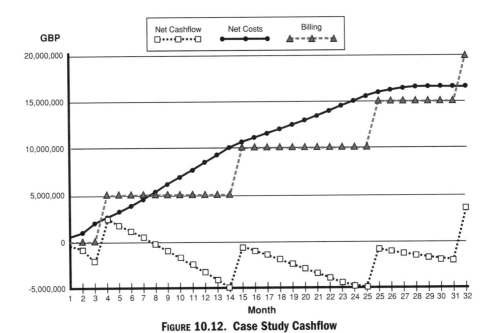

FIGURE **10.12. Case Study Cashflow**

ESTIMATION EFFORT

It took around six weeks to undertake this estimate. Of that time, all but ten days were spent in trying to understand what the system had to do—in drawing up the list of tasks, and in getting a feel for what each one involved. Constructing the Cost Model took six days, and another four were spent in reviews and revisions.

CHAPTER 11

The Cost Model Template

A good plan today is better than a perfect plan tomorrow.

—George S. Patton

INSTALLATION INSTRUCTIONS

The enclosed CD-ROM will run on any IBM-compatible PC running Microsoft Windows 98 or above. A Web browser such as Microsoft Internet Explorer is needed to install the files. You will need Microsoft Office products Excel 97 and Powerpoint 97, or later versions, in order to view or use the information. Use the following procedure to install the files:

1. Insert the CD into your computer's CD drive.
2. Select "Run" from the "Start" toolbar.
3. In the dialog box type d:\start.htm (or substitute the appropriate letter for your CD drive) and click "OK." It is not necessary to connect to the Internet.
4. Read the licence agreement and click "Accept" if you are happy with the conditions of use.
5. Select which file to copy from the following:
   a. **Cost Model Template**. The blank template for use in costing and planning your own projects. This is in Microsoft Excel 97 format.
   b. **Cost Model Case Study**. The complete Case Study described in this book, using the template above.

    c. **Cost Model Simple Example**. The smaller example used in the main text of this book, again using the template.

    d. **IT Project Estimation Diagrams**. Other figures from this book, as a Microsoft Powerpoint 97 presentation. There are no licence restrictions on this file.

6. Select the location on your PC or network where you wish to copy the selected file. In the case of the Cost Model files, Excel may warn you if you wish to enable macros; in fact, the worksheets do not contain any macros, so they may be disabled.

7. The file may then be examined or used, subject to the licence conditions.

LICENCE TERMS AND CONDITIONS

The Cost Model template on the CD-ROM is copyrighted and its use is subject to the licence terms below. Unless you have an individually signed licence, your use of the template signifies your agreement with these terms.

If you do not accept the terms, do not break the seal on the media envelope and return the book to its place of purchase for a refund.

If you are the owner of this book, you may copy and use the Cost Model template, modify the template, and incorporate the template into your own systems and procedures provided that:

1. Copies of the Cost Model template, whether in original, modified, or incorporated form, contain this original copyright notice.

2. The Cost Model template, whether in original, modified, or incorporated form, is available for use either

    a. on no more than three CPUs or

    b. by no more than three users

3. The Cost Model template is not redistributed for commercial gain, whether in original, modified, or incorporated form.

4. The Cost Model template is not installed on a computer Web server or anonymous ftp directory from which it could be downloaded or copied by unlicensed users, whether in original, modified, or incorporated form.

Any other use of the template is a violation of its licence. In using the Cost Model template, you acknowledge and accept this. The template may be individually licenced for use outside these terms and conditions on application to paul.coombs@itprojectestimation.com.

DISCLAIMER OF WARRANTY

The Cost Model template is furnished "as is." The author of this book and its publisher make no warranties, expressed or implied, that the template is free of error, is consistent with any particular standard of merchantability, or that it will meet your requirements for any particular application.

The author of this book and its publisher accept no responsibility for any mathematical or technical limitations of the procedures and functions that make up the Cost Model template. It should not be relied on for solving a problem whose incorrect solution could result in injury to a person or loss of property.

Neither the author of this book nor its publisher shall in any event be liable for any damages, whether direct or indirect, special or general, consequential or incidental, arising from use of the Cost Model template. Your use of the template is entirely at your own risk.

UPDATES TO THE TEMPLATE

Improvements or corrections to the Cost Model template can be downloaded from http://www.itprojectestimation.com. This site also lists the changes made since the previous version and contains other information that may be of interest to readers of this book. Comments on the template and suggestions for improvement are welcomed.

USING THE TEMPLATE

The Cost Model template is a Microsoft Excel 97 workbook. You may change it to suit your own taste, or your organisation's conventions, as you wish, in accordance with the licence agreement above. However, I suggest that you become thoroughly familiar with the template as supplied, or there is a risk that the model will show incorrect calculations. You will need a reasonable level of familiarity with Excel if you are intending to alter the way the model works, although there are no macros.

These notes can also be found in the workbook itself, under the "Notes" tab.

At the bottom of the screen, tabs give access to the following individual sheets:

- **Header**—general information about the project
- **Tasks**—the list of tasks with the base estimate, task contingency, and

project-wide contingency values. Also, when each task will be tackled during the project

- **StaffCosts**—the staff needed for the project, when they will be utilised, and their daily rates
- **CapitalCosts**—items other than staff that will be purchased by the project, and when these costs will be incurred
- **OngoingCosts**—depreciation of capital cost items, and the running costs for the system, such as operations, data preparation, and maintenance
- **RiskAnalysis**—project-wide risks, how they will be managed, and the contingency allowance made
- **Summary**—all the project costs and the final total
- **Cashflow**—billing details, and the monthly profit and loss predicted for the project
- **PriceBreakdown**—allocation of the cost between different elements of the project
- **EarnedValue**—tracking of the project as it proceeds
- **Scratchpad**—an area for defining your own variables as input to the model

In all the sheets, the cells are coloured as follows:

- **Gray** cells are the background and not usually changed.
- **White** cells are for values or text to be input by the user.
- **Pale yellow** cells are values calculated by the spreadsheet.
- **Blue** cells are values carried forward from other sheets or calculations that include such values.
- **Bright yellow** cells highlight risk or contingency values between 20 and 40 percent. These default limits can be found in the "Scratchpad" sheet and altered if required.
- **Bright red** cells highlight risk or contingency values greater than 40 percent.

A red triangle in the corner of a cell shows that there is some help or other note appended. Hold the cursor over the cell to see the text. Owing to an undocumented feature in Microsoft Excel, the size and position of these notes is somewhat unpredictable. If the note is not completely visible, right-click the cell and select "Edit Comment" and then manipulate the notes window until the text is fully visible. If you no longer wish to see the notes, select "Tools", "Options", and then "View" and then choose "None" under "Comments."

There are a number of checks that the model is consistent. Failed checks are shown by red figures appearing, usually in totals. The note appended to the cell in question, or its heading, will describe the values being compared. For fuller details, select the cell, and choose "Format" and then "Conditional Formatting."

There are a number of features of the model that are not used by all projects, so are normally in hidden rows and columns. These can be revealed by "Format", "Row" (or "Column"), and "Unhide." Hidden text is blue by default, so you may like to change this to black. All the hidden features are described below.

Some features of Excel may be selected by the user in order to simplify use of the Cost Model. The "Freeze Panes" option under "Window" allows, for example, the task names to remain in view while you are working on the Task Plan. From the "Customise" option under "View", buttons can be added to the toolbar to allow easy insertion and deletion of rows and columns.

The workbook contains more rows and columns than will be needed for all but the largest projects. Excess rows and columns (e.g., tasks or months) can be removed once the model is complete. However, this will sometimes affect other sheets containing copies of that information—a problem usually indicated by "#REF!" appearing. The sheets containing the copied information must also have the corresponding rows or columns removed. As a safety measure, whenever you add or remove rows or columns you should check that all the formulae for totals are correct.

If you wish to change a sheet, you will want to restore the gridlines and row/column headers—this can be done by selecting "Tools," "Options," and then "View".

Header

This can be changed in accordance with your own procedures for numbering projects, signoff, and so on.

Tasks

The amount of project-level contingency estimated in terms of days is carried forward from the Risk Analysis. Adjust the project contingency percentage (white cell) so the amount allowed is the same as this.

You can create subtotals for project phases, subsystems, and so on by revealing all the hidden rows and columns. By default, the tasks can be assigned to categories labelled A to J, as shown in Figure 11.1.

Category	Base Days	Task Cont. %	Task Cont. Days	Project Cont.	Check
A					
B					
C					
D					
E					
F					
G					
H					
I					
J					

FIGURE 11.1. Task Subtotals

In the normally hidden column labelled "Category", you should assign each task to one of the ten categories by entering a letter from A to J—for example, all the tasks for Phase 1 could be categorised as "A." Then the totals for Category A at the top will show the totals for Phase 1. The label for this totals row can be changed to "Phase 1" without harm.

StaffCosts

Staff rates may be imported or copied from your organisation's Rate Book if you have one. The "Average Rate" is calculated by taking the total number of days and dividing it into the total staff costs. You can create subtotals for specific teams, types of staff, and so on. The procedure is the same as described for the creation of subtotals on the Tasks sheet. Hidden columns to the right of the "Rate" column allow two further rates to be entered for each staff member, as in Figure 11.2. This allows increases if, for example, the project crosses a year boundary and rates are reviewed at each year end. Enter the expected new rate and the month at which it should start to be applied.

CapitalCosts

The amount of project-level contingency estimated in terms of money is carried forward from the Risk Analysis. Adjust the project contingency percentage (white cell) so the amount allowed is the same as this.

Rate	Rate 2	Start	Rate 3	Start
500	525	Jan-03	550	Jan-04

FIGURE 11.2. Alternative Staff Rates

Items can be either depreciated or included in the initial project costs, but not both. In the totals section, the word "Warning!" appears if the item costs do not equal the depreciated amounts plus the values distributed over the project months.

For depreciated costs, it is assumed that the item is totally written off over the assigned period—that is, it has no scrap value. This is usually the case for computer equipment. If the scrap value is significant, add a further column for this, and depreciate a reduced total value over the desired period.

OngoingCosts

Items on this sheet are either staff (e.g., operations or data preparation staff) or other ongoing costs (e.g., hardware maintenance). There are separate sections for each. Staff time should be calculated in days per year for each role, and the appropriate rate inserted. Other items should be entered in terms of their cost per year. Hidden rows in the totals section allow the ongoing costs to be inflated annually, as shown in Figure 11.3. Enter a figure for "Annual Inflation" and the totals for all items, other than the depreciation of capital costs, will be increased yearly.

RiskAnalysis

Variables associated with the calculation of a suitable weighting for each risk can be found in the Scratchpad sheet and in hidden columns at the right of the Risk Analysis sheet. The algorithm is as follows:

1. According to the user entries of L, M, or H for "Probability", "Detection", and "Impact", assign a weighting value taken from *low_weight*, *med_weight*, or *high_weight* respectively (default values are 1, 3, and 7).

	Total	2002	2003	2004	2005	2006	2007
Depreciation of Capital Costs							
Other Ongoing Costs							
Annual Inflation							
Other Ongoing Costs (With Inflation)							
Total Ongoing Costs							

FIGURE **11.3. Inflation of Ongoing Costs**

2. Place the weight in *p_assessment*, *d_assessment*, or *i_assessment* for "Probability", "Detection", and "Impact" respectively.
3. Add the three weights and place in *total_weight*.
4. Assess this total as a proportion of the maximum possible as held in *max_weight* (default = *high_weight* × 3 = 21).
5. Allot a final weighting as this proportion of *max_risk* (default 75 percent) and place it in the "Overall" field.

The "Overall" value is used to modify the maximum days and cost that are assigned to the risk in order to obtain an appropriate contingency allowance.

Summary

Totals are shown quarterly. Monthly totals can simply be obtained from the other sheets.

Cashflow

To determine the project price, you can enter a mark-up on the cost, and the spreadsheet will determine the price (total of "Income"). Alternatively, you may have decided on a price, which can be entered in the "Total Income" cell (the mark-up will remain blank). The billing schedule should add up to 100 percent. The sheet will determine the amount of each bill. Hidden rows can be used to enter interest earned or received, as in Figure 11.4. Enter the interest rate that you will pay for borrowed money, and the rate that you will receive for credit amounts. These rates will be applied monthly according to whether the cashflow is negative or positive.

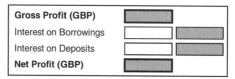

FIGURE 11.4. Interest on Cashflow

PriceBreakdown

The "Ref" and "Task" columns are brought forward from the Tasks sheet. If rows have been added or removed from this, you may need to repair the PriceBreakdown sheet before using it. Check that the totals include all the relevant rows.

The PriceBreakdown sheet should be used as follows:

1. Enter the price or cost that you wish to distribute between the various tasks into the cell labelled "Cost to be Attributed" (*Breakdown_Price*). This may be taken from the Cashflow or Summary sheets—e.g. *Our_Price* or *Initial_Costs_Total*.
2. Enter "T" (no other value) into the "Cost Element" column for all the tasks that you wish to be included in the price breakdown.
3. The SUMIF function is used to determine totals for these values as *Breakdown_Cost_Elements*, and for all other tasks as *Breakdown_Other_Tasks*.
4. The number of days for all tasks shown with a "T" is weighted by the value *Breakdown_Other_Tasks* ÷ *Breakdown_Cost_Elements*.
5. The weighted number of days is used to allocate the *Breakdown_Price* among the selected tasks.

This sheet is very likely to be altered, to incorporate the individual elements that you wish to break down or sum, or the amount of information you wish to reveal. You may wish to use subtotals from the Tasks sheet, or to take more account of the capital costs.

EarnedValue

The "Ref" and "Task" columns, and the number of days planned for each task each month, are brought forward from the Tasks sheet. If rows have been added or removed from this, you may need to repair the EarnedValue sheet before using it. Check that the totals include all the relevant rows.

At the end of each month (or selected time period), and for each task, you should enter the figures for the Budgeted Cost of Work Produced (*BCWP*), indicating how many days of progress have been made. Also enter the Actual Cost of Work Performed (*ACWP*)—usually the time booked by project team members. This may be copied or imported from a project reporting package if you are using one.

Red numbers in the *SV*, *CV*, *SPI*, and *CPI* columns indicate a cost or schedule overrun.

The Estimate At Completion (*EAC*) is calculated as the actual cost to date plus the cost of the remaining work, assuming the current rate of productivity. *ACWS_Total* is the actual cost to date, the remaining work is the Budget at Completion (*BAC*) minus the Earned Value to date (*BCWP_Total*), and *CPI* is the current rate of productivity. So the formula is as follows:

$$EAC = \frac{ACWS\_Total + (BAC - BCWP\_Total)}{CPI}.$$

This is just one of a number of possible formulae for *EAC*. In their book *Earned Value Project Management*, Quentin Fleming and Joel Koppelman say there are "somewhere close to twenty." For example, it could be argued that the current rate of progress, as represented by *SPI*, should also be represented, in which case the divisor should be ($SPI \times CPI$).

The EarnedValue sheet reflects the current state of the Tasks sheet. If you wish to chart a historical view of project progress, you can make a static copy of the current EarnedValue sheet for every reporting period. To do this, select "Edit" and then "Move or Copy Sheet" then make a copy and give it a new name (e.g., "March 2002"). Now select this whole sheet, copy it to the clipboard, and select "Paste Special" and then "Paste Values." This replaces all variable information with its current static value so that if any of the other sheets are changed, the numbers on this sheet will be unaffected. If you make such a copy every reporting period, you can produce historical charts—for example, to examine the effectiveness of your re-planning processes or to see the trends in *CPI* and *SPI*.

Scratchpad

This is used to create variables specific to a particular Cost Model. The variables can then be used in formulae elsewhere in the workbook. The values of the variables may be static or derived from other values in the Cost Model. Some examples are as follows:

- currency exchange rates
- on-site allowances
- daily expenses (e.g., travel abroad)

- number of days for a project phase
- number of days for a project subsystem
- staff rates

To create a variable, enter its name, its value or formula, and a comment about what it represents. To define the name to Excel, the simplest method is to copy the "Name" cell to the clipboard, select the "Value" cell, and then paste the name into the "Name" field on the toolbar (where the cell position is usually displayed). Alternatively, select "Insert", "Name", and then Define." The latter sequence can also be used to remove names.

There are some hidden rows containing values that are built in to the default Cost Model. These may be changed but should not be removed.

Diagrams

It is sometimes easier to create a new worksheet, carrying forward the figures that you wish to chart from any of the other sheets. Select the appropriate cells in the new sheet, and choose the "Chart" icon from the Microsoft Excel toolbar. The appearance of diagrams can be altered by right clicking on any element you wish to change.

CHAPTER 12

References and Resources

Additions and modifications to the information in this chapter can be found on http://www.itprojectestimation.com.

PROJECT FAILURE SURVEYS

The *Standish Group "Chaos" Report* is a survey of 8,380 IT projects undertaken by 365 companies. Of these, 16.2 percent came in within time and budget. Of the successful ones, only 42 percent ended with the functionality originally planned. The full report can be found on http://www.scs.carleton.ca/~beau/PM/Standish-Report.html.

The *BCS Review of 2001* contains a survey of 1,027 projects, of which only 12.7 percent were successful. There is an analysis of the reasons for failure, the stage at which failure occurred, and the skills needed in a project team. The review can be found on http://www.bcs.org.uk/review/2001/html/p061.htm.

Boehm (cited below) has a list of major IT projects and their cost overruns. Each project on the list was cancelled after expending up to four times its original budget.

IT PROJECT ESTIMATION IN GENERAL

The **Software Productivity Consortium** provides processes, methods, tools, and services to its members. These include programs for software measurement—see http://www.software.org/.

The **International Software Benchmarking Standards Group** maintains and exploits a repository of international software project metrics to help improve the management of projects through improved estimation and productivity, risk analysis, and benchmarking. Their Web site is at http://www.isbsg.org.au/. They have produced a *Practical Project Estimation Toolkit*, which is marketed by the Cutter Consortium—see http://www.cutter.com/itreports/practical.html.

The **Society of Cost Estimating and Analysis** is a non-profit organization dedicated to improving cost estimating and analysis in government and industry and enhancing the professional competence and achievements of its members. It publishes the *Journal of Cost Analysis & Management* and runs courses leading to professional qualifications. Their Web site is at http://sceaonline.net.

Estimating Software Costs by Capers Jones (McGraw–Hill, ISBN: 0079130941) is currently out of print. Capers Jones founded Software Productivity Research, who market the KnowledgePLAN tool; he has authored many other books and papers on estimation and software engineering.

Making the Software Business Case: Improvement by the Numbers by Donald Reifer (Addison-Wesley, ISBN: 0201728877) looks at both sides of the coin—presenting the business case for an IT project in terms of costs *and* benefits. It shows how the numbers can be presented in ways that decision-makers expect and understand.

FUNCTION POINT ANALYSIS

The definitive article is A. J. Albrecht and J. E. Gaffney, *Software Function, Source Lines of Code, and Development Effort Prediction: A Software Science Validation. IEEE Transactions in Software Engineering*, November 1983.

Function Point Analysis by David Garmus and David Herron (Addison-Wesley, ISBN: 0201699443) is an easier read and the best place to start if you want to learn all the rules for counting Function Points.

Boehm (cited below) also gives an outline of the "Mark I" process.

The so-called backfiring table, which allows you to convert Function Points to lines of code for various languages, is also provided by Boehm. The very latest version is available to subscribers to the services offered by Software Productivity Research. See http://www.spr.com/products/programming.htm for details and a comprehensive warning as to the pitfalls of applying such a simplistic approach.

Software Sizing and Estimating: Mk II Function Point Analysis by Charles Symons (Wiley, ISBN: 0471929859) provides full details of Mark II Function Points.

Controlling Software Projects: Management, Measurement, and Estimation by Tom DeMarco (Prentice Hall, ISBN: 0131717111) is the book for the Bang methodology.

Capers Jones' *Applied Software Measurement: Assuring Productivity and Quality* covers the calculation of Feature Points and assesses these against other Function Point metrics. This book is currently unavailable.

Object Points are described in *An Empirical Test of Object-Based Output Measurement Metrics in a Computer Aided Software Engineering (CASE) Environment* by R. Banker, R. Kauffman, and R. Kumar, *Journal of Management Information Systems* (1994).

The **Common Software Metrics International Consortium** is responsible for the definition of Cosmic Full Function Points (COSMIC-FFP). Their Web site is at http://www.cosmicon.com/ and shows where the *Measurement Manual*, which defines how to calculate the metric, can be downloaded.

The **International Function Point Users Group** holds conferences, courses, and workshops and refines the counting rules. Their Web site is at http://www.ifpug.org/.

The **Software Engineering Institute** (SEI)—http://www.sei.cmu.edu/—has many articles on software measurement. The checklist for determining what is or is not a "line of code" is called *Software Size Measurement: A Framework for Counting Source Statements* by Robert E. Park and can be downloaded from this site. SEI are also responsible for the Capability Maturity Model (CMM) to evaluate the quality of an organisation's development processes.

PARAMETRIC MODELS AND COCOMO

The bible for COCOMO users is *Software Cost Estimation with COCOMO II* by Barry W Boehm et al. (Prentice Hall, ISBN: 0130266922).

The definitive COCOMO Web site is at the **University of Southern California's Centre for Software Engineering**. Here you will find free support software, details of conferences, calibration initiatives, a bibliography, and much more. The URL is http://sunset.usc.edu/research/cocomoii/.

NASA's *Parametric Cost Estimating Handbook* gives a high-level view of the need for estimation, and describes processes, methodologies, and risks. See http://www.jsc.nasa.gov/bu2/PCEHHTML/pceh.htm.

The **International Society of Parametric Analysts** specialise in parametric models of all types, not just for software, but also for economics, civil engineering, and other disciplines. Their Web site is at http://www.ispa-cost.org/.

COMMERCIALLY AVAILABLE TOOLS

Tool	Vendor	Website
COSTAR	Softstar Systems	http://www.softstarsystems.com/
ESTIMATE Professional	Software Productivity Centre	http://www.spc.ca/
SAGE	Software Engineering Inc.	http://www.seisage.com/
SLIM	Quantitative Software Management	http://www.qsm.com/index.html
PRICE	Price Systems	http://www.pricesystems.com/
SEER	Galorath Inc.	http://www.gaseer.com/
KnowledgePlan	Software Productivity Research	http://www.spr.com/
CostXpert	Cost Xpert Group Inc	http://www.costxpert.com/
Estimacs	Computer Associates	http://www.cai.com/
ObjectMetrix	Tassc	http://www.tassc-solutions.com/

Measures for Excellence: Reliable Software on Time, Within Budget by Lawrence H. Putnam (Yourdon, ISBN 0135676940) is a description of the model behind the SLIM tool. *Software Project Cost and Schedule Estimating: Best Practices* by William H. Roetzheim and Reyna A. Beasley (Prentice Hall, ISBN: 0136820891) describes the CostXpert tool and includes a trial copy. A review of the CostXpert and KnowledgePlan tools from *Information Week* magazine can be found on http://www.informationweek.com/717/17olerr.htm.

The *NVC Method of Software Project Estimation* is a radical new approach that takes considerably less time and is probably just as accurate as many more sophisticated techniques—see http://www.tribalsmile.com/nvc.

RISK AND CONTINGENCY MANAGEMENT

The following books provide descriptions of possible risks and the ways in which they may be controlled: *Assessment and Control of Software Risks* by Capers Jones (Yourdon Press, ISBN: 0137414064) and *Managing Software Quality and Business Risk* by Martyn Ould (Wiley, ISBN: 047199782X).

Critical Chain by Eliyahu M. Goldratt (Avebury, ISBN: 0566080389) is written as a novel, albeit one where the central characters have long conversations about project management technique. The same is true of his best-known work, *The Goal* (Gower Publishing Limited, ISBN: 0566074184), which while not directly relevant to IT projects, has insight into ways in which all processes and systems can be improved. If you prefer textbooks to novels, *Project Management in the Fast Lane* by Robert C. Newbold (St. Lucie Press, ISBN: 1574441957) is an excellent guide to Goldratt's methods and how they can be applied in the real world. Related Web sites are listed on http://www.goldratt.co.uk/links.html.

REVIEWS

The Wideband–Delphi review method is described in *Software Engineering Economics* by Barry Boehm (Prentice Hall, ISBN: 0-13-822122-7). A summary can also be found in an article entitled *Stop Promising Miracles* by Karl E. Weigers—see http://www.processimpact.com/articles/delphi.html. Weigers' *Peer Reviews in Software: A Practical Guide* (Addison-Wesley, ISBN: 0201734850) covers the review process throughout the development life cycle.

PROJECT MANAGEMENT

Earned Value Project Management by Quentin W. Fleming and Joel M. Koppelman (Project Management Institute, ISBN: 1880410273) is a brief, readable but comprehensive guide to this technique.

Information on Microsoft Project is obtainable from http://www.microsoft.com/office/project/.

ON-LINE BIBLIOGRAPHIES

The **Data & Analysis Center for Software** is a U.S. Department of Defense software information clearinghouse. Many estimation resources can be found on their Web site—http://www.dacs.dtic.mil/.

There is an extensive bibliography of literature relating to Function Point Analysis at the Web site of the University of Quebec's Software Engineering Management Research Laboratory—see http://www.lrgl.uqam.ca/fp/fp.html.

Relevant references can also be found at the website of the University of Southern California's Centre for Software Engineering—see http://sunset.usc.edu/research/COCOMOII/cost_bib.html.

OTHERS

Anything written by Tom Demarco is entertaining and insightful. In particular, *Why Does Software Cost So Much?: And Other Puzzles of the Information Age* (Dorset House, ISBN: 093263334X) delves into the sociological and psychological drivers behind IT projects. I don't know how to incorporate them into your estimates, but such factors as fear of failure, losing face, rigid rules, and organisational traditions are fundamental to the success of any team and any project.

The Mythical Man-Month by Frederick P. Brooks (Addison-Wesley, ISBN: 0201835959) draws its examples from a long-gone age, but its fundamental points are still as applicable as ever—the last 10 percent of a software project may take more resources than all those used so far, and adding resources to a failing project will only make it finish even later.

All books by Douglas R. Hofstadter are inspirational and challenging. Specifically, his essay *On Number Numbness* discusses just how hard it is to envisage what large numbers really mean. It can be found in *Metamagical Themas: Questing for the Essence of Mind and Pattern* (Basic Books, ISBN: 0465045669).

And finally, Edward Yourdon's *Deathmarch* (Prentice Hall, ISBN: 0130146595), while not especially about estimation, does tell you how to survive projects with impossible staffing levels, schedules, budgets, or features. Let's hope you don't need it.

Index